THE VALLEY OF THE SHADOW

The Valley of the Shadow

An account of Britain's worst mining disaster: the Senghenydd Explosion

by

JOHN H. BROWN

ALUN BOOKS
Port Talbot
2009

To
Clarice, Hilary, Catherine and Frances
and for
the womenfolk of the mining communities of the Aber Valley and the South Wales coalfield, whose harsh experiences taught them the true cost of coal.

'O what is man that coal should be so careless of him
And what is coal that so much blood should be upon it?'

Idris Davies (Gwalia Deserta)

ISBN 0 907117 06 6

Published by
Alun Books, 3 Crown Street, Port Talbot

First published 1981
Second Edition, reset with minor corrections 2009

Set in 9/12pt Imperial

Typeset and Printed in Great Britain by
Andreas Haaf & Son, Port Talbot
Bound by Abbey Bookbinders, Cardiff

CONTENTS

Foreword

THERE ARE three Cs that come immediately to mind when I think of my childhood homes in the Rhymney and Aber valleys:-

Coal — the economic power house which drove the early prosperity of the area.
Community — the towns and villages where friends and neighbours worked and played together to forge a uniquely 'valleys' lifestyle.
Communication — the love of words and song to express principle, conviction and emotion which is part of our Welsh heritage.

My father's book, The Valley of the Shadow, draws on all three and grew out of his desire to tell the story of the people of the Aber valley involved in the great disaster of 1913. Working among the community in the early 1960s, as manager of the Ministry of Pensions and National Insurance he met some of the survivors of the explosion and the families of those who were not so lucky on that terrible day. Using their memories and his own painstaking research he was determined to paint a picture not only of the suffering and heroism which naturally attend such a catastrophe but also the roles of the wider cast of characters involved — owners, politicians, union officials, barristers and lawyers.

The world depicted in this book has long changed and disappeared, but it is possible to understand both the mechanisms which led to such a terrible disaster and the price paid by the community so dramatically and devastatingly affected. The virtues and vices which lie embedded in the narrative are timeless and universal and so the story of the Senghenydd Explosion will always be relevant.

Researching and writing this book occupied most of my father's all too brief retirement, but I know that he felt it was time well spent. I hope that in reading it you will understand something of the heroism, courage and suffering of this small mining community which compelled him to put pen to paper.

My thanks to all the team of enthusiastic and talented workers at the Heritage Centre in Senghenydd and at Alun Books who have made it possible to publish this second edition. We all hope, along with its author, that you find this a book which both informs your mind and stirs you heart.

Hilary Reed (nee Brown)

Author's Note

THE STORY I have striven to tell here had its origins in my accidental association with the people of this mining valley when I came to work among them in 1959. As a boy in the South Wales of the 1920s and 1930s I had seen the effects of unemployment and depression, but here the people I met daily had faced communal calamity and disaster long before the depression years brought their own peculiar and additional troubles. Their struggle against extreme adversity was only suggested or implied in snippets of conversation but, with the passage of time, I became more and more aware of the enormity of the suffering they had borne — and borne with a silent independence and stoical fortitude. But there was no one place where I could, for myself, read the basic facts behind their story. For this reason I was moved to uncover these details myself.

My researches led me from 1913 back to 1901 and earlier with numerous sidetracks into intervening years to pick up influences and actions which were all relevant — in my eyes — to the final act of tragedy. I was led from newspaper reports to Coroners' inquests, from reports of Royal Commissions and Departmental Committees to Acts of Parliament and regulations, and from reports by Mines Inspectors to all kinds of published material which might provide information relevant to the dire experiences of this small community. Yet in following this trail always I had to return to this valley for its people's story — because it is essentially their story, even though many of its elements are true for all the mining communities of South Wales.

In deciding to write their story I was moved to bring together, as an entity, all these facts and details, including personal accounts and reminiscences from survivors and local inhabitants — so that others might read this piece of recent social history. As such it is a tribute to the moral fibre of the people of this valley — and it may help many to understand the camaraderie and independent spirit of coal mining communities.

In my efforts I have received assistance and information from a great many people, both in this valley and elsewhere. In particular I am indebted to Messrs. William Hyatt, Bert Walters, Evan Moore and Theo Lewis for the time they so freely gave to recount their experiences in the disaster and their memory of this valley nearly seventy years ago. As octogenarians all, their lucid description and clear recall of the happenings on a day long ago gave form and extent to the shock and trauma engendered by a disaster in which they were participants. To these four — and the many others who added to my sum total of information and local detail — my warm thanks.

I am grateful, too, for the assistance I received from the staffs of the County of South Glamorgan's Central Library at Cardiff, the County of Mid Glamorgan's Branch Library at Pontypridd, the National Coal Board Library at Llanishen, the National Library of Wales at Aberystwyth, the Newspaper Library of the British Library at Colindale, the Records Office for the Counties of Glamorgan, and the Industry Section of the National Museum of Wales.

Newspapers, Libraries and the National Museum of Wales were most helpful in tracing and allowing me to use appropriate photographs. Mrs A. Holder, Mrs K. Moore, Mrs E. Prendergast, Mr Evan Moore and Mr D. R. Lewis also loaned their treasured photographs.

I thank them all. I appreciate the permission so kindly and readily given by: –

- Collins. Publishers — to quote the thoughts of Sarah Burton from 'South Riding' by Winifred Holtby.
- Professor B. F. Duckham and Mrs Helen Duckham to quote the telling passage on the effects of mining disasters from their book 'Great Pit Disasters — Great Britain — 1700 to the Present Day.'
- Mrs Dorothy Morris, sister of the late Idris Davies, to quote two lines from stanza IV from his 'Gwalia Deserta.'

To Alan Izzard I am indebted for the excellent plans of the mine, etc. he produced to illustrate the text. The efforts of Miss Pauline Jones in tracing legislation and other documents was a great help and saved me a great deal of time.

Finally I owe a major debt of gratitude to Mrs Jean Jackson who, over a long time, has steadfastly converted my execrable handwriting into a readable typescript whilst eliminating inconsistencies and adjusting inaccuracies.

I realise only too well how much help I have received from all these — thank you.

JOHN H. BROWN
Glyn Elyrch, Penyrheol, Caerphilly
February 1980

List of Illustrations

PLANS

Chapter 1

The Valley of the Shadow

IT IS A little valley — far too small for all the grief it was once called upon to contain and bear. Yet outwardly there is little obvious evidence of this and nothing readily distinguishes it from the bigger and better known mining valleys of South Wales.

Sheep browse on its hillsides and sometimes wander down into the villages. There with all the imperturbable indifference of India's sacred cows they rummage in dustbins, ravage the gardens and befoul the streets. These streets follow the line of the valley and in places seem to climb like rows of knitting up its mountain slopes.

As in all these valleys life here has clotted around the winding gear of the coal mines which have been the source of its daily bread and, quite often, the cause of its poverty and suffering. In this valley one colliery exists but only because its winding gear is still there. The absence of activity around the pit-head is a sign of another colliery name recorded on the National Coal Board's death roll due to rationalisation. The grey black tip dominating the mountain top is now neglected by its former attendant aerial buckets which spewed their rubbish onto it to provide the sustenance for its growth. Only the ropeway gantries remain like silent sentinels to guard the monster they once served.

There are other tips, from workings long closed, whose blackness is being softened by the green mould of moss and grass nature employs to cover the mistakes and intrusion of man. Quarries scar the hillsides to show where the valley's older buildings had their origin. But there is evidence of other scars, also. Here and there derelict and shuttered shops remind one that this area has suffered depression, unemployment and poverty which spread like ringworm from the collieries to affect all aspects of valley life. But prosperity has left its mark too. This is reflected in the imposing facades and opulent size of the public houses — easily the valley's largest buildings.

The religious fervour of past years is apparent in the number, size and austere splendour of the chapels with their impressive facades and vaulted windows — and present materialism and religious indifference in their obvious neglect. The Workmen's Institutes which once, with the chapels, were the cultural foci of these communities still occupy a central position in the villages. But, whereas they were the freedom road of learning for many a miner trying to break out of the bondage of coal, they have lost their cultural and educational purpose. Now, due to financial starvation, they have deteriorated into bingo halls or been converted into community centres.

The railway line is closed and the stations have been demolished to make way for council flats, bungalows and modern housing. The railway embankments and cuttings are now an unofficial playground for children or a repository for the metal and plastic rubbish which modern society spawns and spreads.

The drab exteriors of most of the old stone built houses have been brightened with colourful fresh paint, for the grime associated with coal does not intrude into the homes of these mining folk. They are a proud and houseproud people and this shows in the bright exteriors of their homes and the spotless welcoming interiors. As valley folk they recognise the visual welcome of a cheerful fire and in many homes a bright coal fire burns merrily beneath a mantelpiece supporting an altar-like array of shining brass candlesticks.

Like villages in other mining valleys these have their village squares and war memorials around which the old and the young commune and sit — the old to recall coal seams now worked out and workmates and incidents long departed — the young to ogle, whistle and sport with all the brash nonchalance of their years.

In the valley the only truly level areas are those specifically designed for the recreation of the older and younger sections of the community. The old have their bowling greens where the men pirouette and posture to influence the speed and bias of the wood to caress the 'jack.' The young men have their rugby pitch where Welsh fervour reaches religious revival intensity on winter Saturday afternoons as the devotees strain to graduate to the highest honour they acknowledge — the dragon's blood red jersey of the Welsh Rugby XV.

The villages have their ambulance halls emblazoned with the Maltese Cross insignia of the Order of St John. They are a strong but silent witness to a mining community's ready recognition that immediate and first aid in calamity originates in the community itself. The lesson of the good

Samaritan and 'who is my neighbour?' has been taught and learned in these halls by miners, their siblings and their womenfolk so that the rudiments of aid and comfort could enable them to be a ready help in trouble. Over the years these halls have been veritable community centres and served as places of worship, for lectures, committee meetings and, as a sad ultimate service to the village communities in their time of greatest need, as a mortuary.

The living gossip and shop in the valley's Commercial Street and High Street and around the village squares, while the dead of the valley are buried in its little churchyard high up in a fold of the mountain and in its newer cemetery nestling behind a high wall on the main road leading out of the valley.

And there, all similarity with other Welsh mining valleys ends.

For if any discerning gleaner of epitaphs wanders into this valley's little cemeteries at Eglwysilan and Penyrheol he is soon struck by the frequency with which one date appears on the tombstones he sees. Again and again it is inscribed above the graves of boys, young men and old men and above the names of father, son, grandson, brother and brother-in-law.

What holocaust flamed through this valley causing so many men to die on the same day? Commercial Street, High Street and all the other streets in the valley give no clue to the answer. The houses and shops are expressionless and mute and do not record the happenings and grief they witnessed and encompassed.

Yet, on one day, 45 men died from this Commercial Street; 35 men died from High Street; 19 men died from Stanley Street, while in the four rows of houses of Woodland, Phillips, Graig and Cenydd Terraces, known locally as 'the Four Terraces,' 56 men died.

This toll of death in one day numbs the senses with its enormity but its searing starkness and poignancy only becomes apparent when one appreciates how individual houses were affected.

In 40 Ilan Road the father Benjamin Priest, age 36, and his two sons, Jimmy, age 14 and Tommy, age 16, died together; from 20 Caerphilly Road the father, George Henry Downes, age 43, with his two sons, George and Tom, age 20 and 19 respectively, all died; in 61 Caerphilly Road three brothers, Morgan, Thomas and George Edwards all died; in 68 Commercial Street Mrs Elizabeth Twining, widowed a year earlier, lost her three sons, John Edward, age 28, James, age 16 and Evan, age 14.

And this is repeated in house after house after house. Catastrophe and attendant grief stalked through the streets of this little valley and touched most of its homes. For example in a typical cluster of houses in Commercial

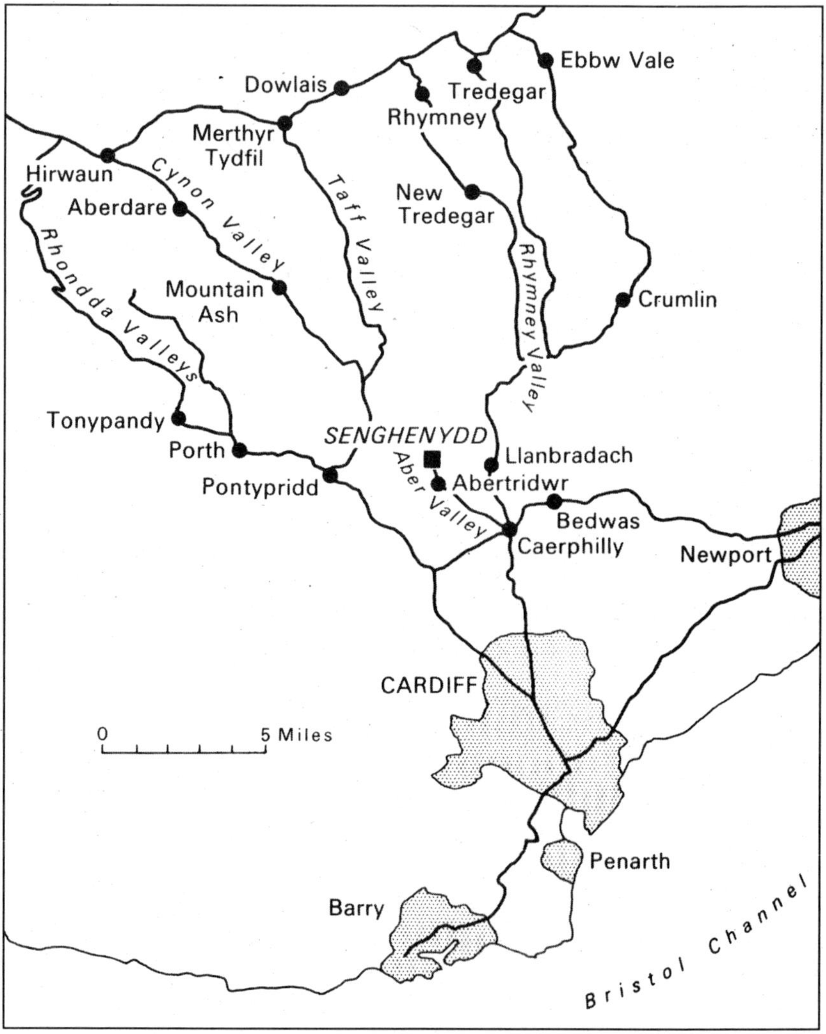

1. Senghenydd and the Aber Valley

Street the death toll was:-

No. 159: 3 dead
No. 164: 2 dead
No. 165: 1 dead
No. 167: 1 dead
No. 169: 2 dead
No. 171: 1 dead
No. 176: 1 dead

This meant that nearly every home and every family throughout the valley was affected through blood ties, friendship or neighbourliness by this pall of sorrow.

In the plague of Pharaoh's valley of the Nile the Angel of Death claimed only the first born, but here he was much more rapacious and took the first born, mid born, last born and head of the family with wanton and indiscriminate equanimity.

Of the 439 men who died that day, 185 were in the middle ages of thirty to fifty, 162 were in their twenties, 63 were in their teens, including 10 sixteen year olds, 5 fifteen year olds and 8 boys of fourteen years of age. One can only guess how many today, at that age, would still be at school and protected by classroom walls from a death that cheated them of a life unlived.

For a clue as to what happened one must return to the village graveyards where the epitaphs above the dead are now the only visible witness to the disaster which shattered this valley community. The carved and leaden words on the gravestones show that each and every one of these boys and men died on the 14th October 1913 and some go on to declare the day was Tuesday.

Every epitaph silently and stonily records, in Welsh, . . . *'Bu farw yn Nanchwa Senghenydd,'* or in English, . . . *'Died in the Senghenydd Explosion.'*

This little valley is the Aber Valley, some ten miles north of Cardiff, with its villages of Abertridwr and Senghenydd.

And the disaster which stalked its streets and claimed its menfolk was the explosion at the Lancaster Pit of the Universal Colliery at Senghenydd on Tuesday, 14th October 1913.

As the worst mining disaster of all time in Britain among miners it is known and recognised, quite simply, as *'The Senghenydd Explosion.'*

Senghenydd and the Universal Colliery in the early 1900s
(permission of the National Museum of Wales)

Chapter 2

There is a divinity that shapes our ends . . .

IN 1913 the Universal Colliery at Senghenydd was owned by the Lewis Merthyr Consolidated Collieries Ltd as part of the vast empire of industrial interests acquired and operated by the first Lord Merthyr of Senghenydd.

Long before he assumed this title, with all its ultimate association with tragedy, grief and attendant recrimination, unseen and powerful pressures seem to have determined the mould of Lord Merthyr's life, his association with the heavy industries of South Wales, his choice of title and, indeed, the inevitability of the Senghenydd explosion.

These pressures emanated from sources as diverse as an ancestor who was an iron master and industrialist, a Welsh chieftain of Norman times, a Scottish Marquess, an astute and enterprising widow whose interest in coal mining earned for herself the title of 'Mother of the Welsh steam coal trade' and the intrinsic burning qualities of Welsh steam coal. Each in their individual way pointed him along the road ultimately leading to the ownership of the Universal Colliery at Senghenydd.

The boy who was to become the owner of the Lewis Merthyr Consolidated Collieries Ltd was born William Thomas Lewis at Abercaniad House, Merthyr Tydfil on 5th August 1837. His father, Thomas William Lewis, was engineer to the Plymouth ironworks and collieries at Merthyr Tydfil and claimed ancestry with the famous Welsh family of Lewis of the Van at Caerphilly. The Lewis family's connections with the iron trade in Merthyr began with Thomas Lewis of the Van. It was he who, at Dowlais, near Merthyr, set up a small furnace which began making iron in 1758. The material for the construction of this furnace was transported by William Lewis, a relative of Thomas Lewis and the great, great grandfather of Lord Merthyr. When the furnace ultimately went into production William Lewis transported the iron it produced. Here the foundations were laid for the

Lewis family's long association with the heavy industries of South Wales.

For the family's links with Senghenydd one needs to go even further back along the Lewis line to the Welsh chieftain, Ifor ap Meurig. Because of his small stature, he was known by the Welsh as 'Ifor Bach' and by the Normans as 'Ifor le Petit.' Ifor's lack of inches was compensated by his courage, guile and resolution. His extensive estates included Senghenydd and he had an impressive retinue of followers and men at arms. He earned his place in history by his successful assault of Cardiff Castle in 1158 when he and his men scaled the walls at night and abducted Earl William, his wife Hawise, and son Robert. These he held to ransom in his hill fortress until the Normans restored the lands which Ifor contended William had unjustly taken from him.

Ifor's foray had its origin in the changes which the passage of time inevitably brought about in the Norman holders of the lordship of Cardiff and Glamorgan.

The first Norman Lord of Glamorgan was Robert Fitzhamon who, as a kinsman and trusted follower of King William, had been granted the lordship of Gloucester. From this base he had led his men across the Severn into Wales where he defeated Iestyn ap Gwrgan, the Welsh Lord of Morgannwg, and established the Lordship of Glamorgan on Iestyn's kingdom. In his march from the Severn into Glamorgan Fitzhamon followed the Roman road from Caerleon and, reaching Cardiff, adopted the derelict Roman fort there as his defensive base. The mediaeval castle was a 'motte and bailey' structure and this became the Norman centre for the area around Cardiff. From here Fitzhamon assigned estates to his knights and administered the rule of law. Outside this feudal area Fitzhamon's influence was largely dependent on the allegiance and trust he could evoke from the Welsh chieftains in the hills. In this he appears to have succeeded because descendants of Iestyn ap Gwrgan and of Einon ap Collwyn, another Welsh chieftain, are known to have held these districts whilst paying fealty to the Glamorgan Lord.

After Fitzhamon's death in 1107 the Lordship of Glamorgan reverted to King Henry I. Henry had an illegitimate son, Robert, who became known as Robert Consul or Robert the Earl. In 1118 Robert came of age and, having already married Fitzhamon's daughter and heiress, it was natural he should assume, in his wife's name, the Honour of Gloucester and the Lordship of Glamorgan and Cardiff. On an unruly border in the face of an aggressive foe, as the king's man, the Lord of Glamorgan had powers far exceeding those of the ordinary barons. Also, as the successor to the conqueror of the area he had nearly complete autonomy and independence in deciding action as necessity dictated. It is fair to record that Robert Consul appeared to use these powers wisely and fairly, granting concessions to the Welsh who, in turn, provided him with a formidable body of auxiliaries when needed. He was well trusted by the king to whom he was devoutly loyal and among the Welsh was well respected and accepted as tolerant, wise and promoting order and justice.

But the old order changed when Robert was succeeded by his son William. He did not display his father's flair for reconciling the Welsh or his ability in resisting them. His brush with Ifor Bach highlights this, as it does, no less, the audacity of Ifor in assaulting Cardiff Castle and kidnapping its Lord, his wife and son to effect the restoration of his estates. Following this foray the strained relations between Ifor and the Earl called for immediate remedy. This was resolved by Ifor being required to pay homage direct to the King — Henry II. As a consequent 'tenant in capite' he ceased to be subject to the Lord of Cardiff. Little wonder Ifor Bach of Senghenydd was an ancestral star at the top of the Lewis family tree or that the title of the Lordship of Senghenydd could hold attraction for a successful industrialist.

As a boy William Lewis was educated at Merthyr in the school run by Taliesin Williams, son of the famous bard and antiquarian Iolo Morgannwg, but he left school at the age of 13 to be articled to his father in the engineering office of the Plymouth Works at Merthyr.

At that time the chief mining engineer to the Marquess of Bute's mineral empire in Glamorgan was V. S. Clark who, in 1855, was looking for a likely assistant to help him with two major projects needed to extend and consolidate the Bute interests. These were the construction of the Bute Docks at Cardiff and the laying of the Rhymney Railway to connect the Bute Ironworks at Rhymney in the north-west corner of Monmouthshire with the port facilities of Cardiff. Clark discussed his need for an assistant with David Williams, licensee of the Greyhound Hotel at Merthyr and partner with a Mr Nixon in the Werfa Colliery. Typical of the nepotism and patronage often apparent in a clannish community like the Welsh, Williams recommended the young Lewis boy and arranged to make the necessary enquiries to get the young engineer to call on Clark.

Lewis was appointed and began working with Clark on the building of the Bute Docks and the Rhymney Railway. This gave him valuable experience and it was inevitable that when Clark died in 1864 he should assume his master's mantle. He was appointed mineral agent to the Bute estate and took over Clark's residence at the Mardy, Aberdare. In the same year he married Miss Anne Rees, the daughter of William Rees of Lletty Shenkin

Collieries in the Cynon Valley. Anne Rees was also the granddaughter of Mrs Lucy Thomas of Waun Wyllt, who became the acknowledged 'Mother of the Welsh Steam Coal Trade.'

In 1828 her husband Robert Thomas opened a coal level at Waun Wyllt, Abercaniad. He died soon after and Mrs Thomas decided to carry on the business with the help of her son William. Through George Insole of Cardiff their coal found an initial market in London and its smokeless properties inspired James Maychurch to come from London in 1830 to seek the source of this smokeless coal. Having tracked it down Maychurch contracted with Mrs Thomas to buy all her output at four shillings (20p) a ton; he sold it in London at eighteen shillings (90p) a ton. This was to be the base from which the Welsh steam coal market grew to become a world-wide trade.

When young Lewis married Anne Rees she brought with her a considerable fortune deriving from her father's and grandmother's mining interests. This enabled her husband to extend his responsibility for managing the Bute estate into the lucrative field of colliery speculation.

He cut his teeth in this sphere on the Bute-Merthyr pits at Treherbert and extended this interest between 1870 and 1880. By gaining control of pits at Coedcae and Hafod in the Lower Rhondda Valley in these years he laid the foundation for the Lewis-Merthyr empire.

In 1880 John Boyle, the trustee to the Bute estate, retired and Lewis took his place. From this position he was able to influence and persuade Lord Bute to improve railway and dock facilities at Cardiff for the export of the coal they were both now winning from the South Wales valleys. In 1882 Parliament passed the Bill for the construction of the Roath Dock at Cardiff and this was built under Lewis' personal supervision and opened in 1887.

In the managerial and ownership field he was equally astute and enterprising in extending and consolidating his interests. In 1864 he had recommended and implemented the formation of a Coal Owners' Mutual Association for the Aberdare Valley, now the Cynon Valley. Experience proved it to be too small in concept and in 1871 it was extended to include the coal owners and iron masters of South Wales as the South Wales and Monmouthshire Coal Owners' Association.

With such a strong combination of owners the path was open for an assault on wages. This followed in 1875 when the owners locked out the miners for five months to enforce a reduction in wages. Resumption of work was only agreed following the acceptance by the miners of a reduction in wages of 12½ per cent and the establishment for the future of a sliding scale of wages regulated by the selling price of coal.

Sir William Thomas Lewis — First Lord Merthyr of Senghenydd *(permission of the National Library of Wales)*

This iniquitous system was to be the source of dissension in South Wales until early into the 1900s. Whilst it operated a decent living wage for miners it could never determine the market value of coal; rather it was a 'cart before the horse' arrangement where the selling price determined wages.

When the price of coal was high the level of wages moved upwards also, but to a level still assuring the coal owners of their profit margin. When the price fell the owners were likely to benefit from increased sales, lower wages and the profits attending greater turnover. Also, as some of the coal owners had fingers in the iron and steel pies, cheap coal reduced their overheads and increased their profits in those industries. To many it seemed the owners were tossing the coin in a 'heads I win, tails you lose' game.

This wages system was administered by a joint committee of representatives of the workmen and the coal owners. The expenses of the workmen's side were met by a contribution of two pence (1p) per month from the individual miner's wages. This paid the miners' agent who, as vice chairman of the joint committee, was in the invidious position of being paid his members' contributions through colliery offices operated by the coal owners.

From 1875 to 1902, for the whole period of the existence of a sliding scale agreement, the miners' agent and vice-chairman was William Abraham, better known by his bardic title of Mabon. Mabon was a staunch supporter of the principle of the sliding scale and this attitude, coupled with his association with Lewis — who was chairman of the joint committee from 1880 to 1899 — gave grounds for allegations that he was a 'boss's man.' There is no doubt at all that Mabon was sincerely motivated by his appraisal of the best interests of his members. They recognised this and elected him member of parliament for Rhondda in 1885. It was his persuasion which won from the owners the privilege of a holiday for miners on the first Monday of each month — a day known throughout the coal field as 'Mabon's Day.'

However, opposition to the wages system and its deleterious effect on trade unionism grew in the coal field and came from Keir Hardie, Sidney and Beatrice Webb and the Miners' Federation of Great Britain. In Monmouthshire, the opposition was led by Risca born William Brace. Brace, as spokesman for the miners of Monmouthshire, also became their MP — but this did not prevent his opposing Mabon's wages policy. His forthright denunciation of the principles of the wage agreement and Mabon's relationship with the owners eventually incited Mabon to take legal action against him for libel. Mabon's action was successful and he was awarded £500 damages against Brace — it was an award that Brace never paid and which Mabon did not press to a conclusion. This prolonged encounter by Brace with the policies and forces of Sir William Thomas Lewis over the sliding scale presaged the later encounter when he was to represent the deceased miners at the inquest and inquiry at Senghenydd.

In 1878 Parliament became extremely concerned about safety in mines and set up a Royal Commission under the chairmanship of Earl Crawford and Balcarres to examine and report on this. Lewis' wide experience of engineering and coal mining made him ideal for appointment to this Commission which sat between February 1879 and March 1886. In his report to Parliament the Chairman paid special tribute to Lewis' valuable assistance and to his practical knowledge of the problems attending the mining of coal.

Between 1878 and 1880 a series of bad explosions caused many deaths and serious distress to miners' dependants. This highlighted the need to establish a fund, to which coal owners and workmen should contribute, to alleviate this distress. For South Wales Lewis recommended the formation of a Monmouthshire and South Wales Permanent Provident Society to meet this special need and this was duly set up.

By now he was acknowledged as a personage of importance and influence in the industrial field and in initiating charitable works. His munificence was in proportion to his fortune and it was a generosity which could not long go unrecognised and unrewarded. In 1885 Queen Victoria acknowledged his works with a knighthood and this was followed by a baronetcy in 1896. In 1911 he was elevated to the peerage when he took the title of Lord Merthyr of Senghenydd.

By 1889 he had begun to explore the possibility of developing the steam coal deposits south of Llanbradach in the Rhymney Valley. This led them to consider working these rich seams from Senghenydd in the adjacent Aber Valley, and just over the mountain from Llanbradach. To mine this coal the Universal Steam Coal Company was set up in 1889 with capital of £100,000 under a directorate of Herbert C. Lewis (Sir William's son), Henry Wm. Martin, Thomas Morel, W. T. Rees and Valentine Trayes. Lewis had already constructed the Rhymney Railway Company's line from Rhymney to Cardiff, so to serve his new pit he needed a railway line from Caerphilly to Senghenydd. The Railway Company obtained Parliamentary consent for this in 1890 and the sinking of the Universal Colliery began in 1891.

In that year a row of one storey huts, roofed and walled with corrugated iron and painted with tar, were hurriedly constructed opposite the site of the colliery. They were built to house the shaft sinkers and the railway construction workers and for years they were known in Senghenydd as 'The Huts.' When the sinking and railway work was completed many of the men found work in the mine opposite their homes. This proximity was to result in the death of six of them in the 1913 explosion.

By 4th December 1895 the Lancaster Pit of the colliery had reached 650 yards and between this and 493 yards depth five workable seams had been uncovered. At the end of another five years 183,600 tons of coal were being won annually from the seams being worked.

The scene was set and the characters had assembled even though they knew not the plot. All that was needed was a dress rehearsal. This was destined to take place in May 1901 when an explosion in the Universal Pit was to give Senghenydd and Abertridwr their first bitter taste of sorrow and misery.

Chapter 3

Backcloth to dusty death

BY MAY 1901 the Universal Colliery had been operating and winning coal from the seams beneath Senghenydd for over five years. The other colliery in the valley — the Windsor Colliery at Abertridwr and about a mile south of Universal — was still in process of being sunk and one of its shafts had just reached the first of the steam coal seams.

At the Senghenydd mine the five seams which were revealed when the 650 yard deep shafts were sunk were the Two Feet Nine Seam at 493 yards, the Four Feet Seam at 507 yards, the Six Feet Seam at 530 yards, the Universal Seam at 535 yards and the Nine Feet Seam at 558 yards.

The two shafts, both 18½ feet in diameter, were 50 yards apart in a line running north and south. The northerly pit was known as the Lancaster pit and its companion, to the south, the York pit. The Lancaster pit was the downcast shaft through which air was taken to ventilate the workings in the mine. The spent air was drawn out of the mine through the return roads in the workings to the upcast shaft of the York pit. This stale air was extracted by a Walker fan, 24 feet in diameter, situated at the surface. Running at a speed of 33 revolutions per minute, which was well within its capacity, the fan circulated about 120,000 cubic feet of air through the mine. This provided adequate ventilation in all the workings.

In the shafts permanent landings had been formed at the Six Feet Seam level of about 530 yards. Levels were driven east and west from this landing in both shafts and, consequently, the main division of the districts worked in the mine was that of the west side and the east side.

The main level into the west side was the Lancaster Level and through this air was conveyed into the five west side districts. These districts were known as No 2 South, Pretoria, Mafeking, Kimberley and Ladysmith. After circulation in these districts the air was drawn out to the York shaft through the Main Return which ran parallel to the Lancaster Level. (See plan on page 24.)

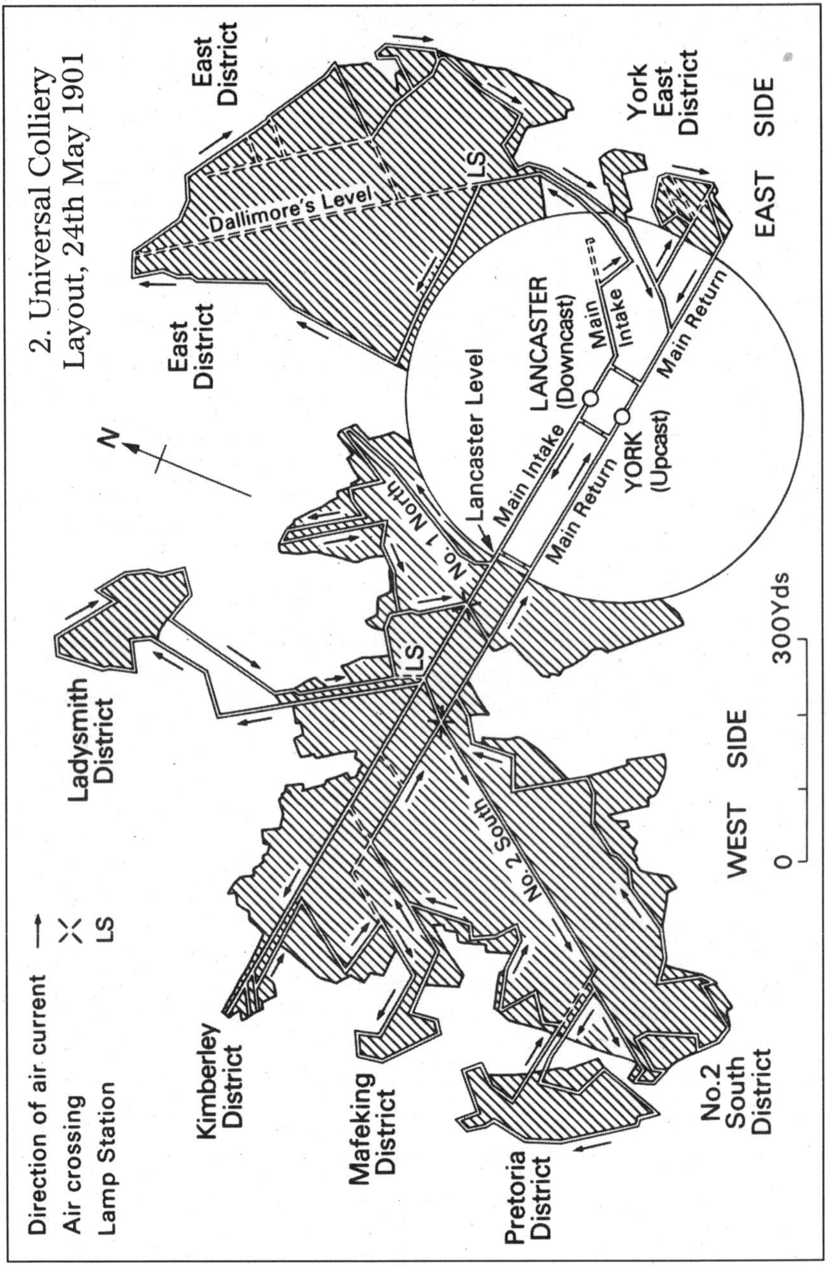

2. Universal Colliery Layout, 24th May 1901

On the east side the main intake level was known as the East Side Main. This carried air into the two east side districts known as the East and York East Districts. Spent air from these workings returned to the York pit via the East York Main Return.

In all districts except the No 2 South, where the Six Feet Seam was being worked, coal was won from the Four Feet Seam. To provide stability and support for the shafts and the surface buildings no coal was worked in the area of a semi-circle of diameter 500 yards around each of the two shafts.

Paradoxically, the Four Feet Seam contained a total thickness of about 6 feet of coal whilst the Six Feet Seam had just over 4 feet of coal in it. The seams were about 23 yards apart in the strata, with the Four Feet uppermost. Both were fairly horizontal and where they undulated did so to the same extent. Where faults or dislocations occurred these brought some areas of the higher Four Feet Seam nearly opposite areas of the lower seam along the lines of dislocation. Working the seams was thus relatively easy and the mine was consequently accepted by colliers as a good one to work in. It was a dry mine where very little water seeped into working places. Because of this a great deal of coal dust was created and this accumulated in the haulage roads along which coal was conveyed to the surface. In time these accumulations were to demonstrate their explosive potential.

Examination and supervision of the workings by firemen and other officials was assigned on a 'ventilating district' basis, as required by the Coal Mines Regulation Act 1887. There were five ventilating districts in the mine. No 1 ventilating district embraced the two districts (i.e. East and York East Districts) on the east side. Of the four ventilating districts on the west side No 2 was the Ladysmith District; No 3 comprised Kimberley and Mafeking together; Pretoria itself was No 4 while No 5 consisted of the workings in the No 2 South District. Oversight of these five ventilating districts lay with eight firemen — four by day and four by night. This provided two firemen for the single ventilating district on the east side and two with responsibility for the four districts in the west.

There was an overman for the day shift and one by night but no under-manager. Instead Edward Shaw, the certificated manager of the colliery, assumed the responsibility normally associated with this post and carried out the daily supervision it required by law.

Shaw had succeeded his father as manager of the colliery on his father's death some ten weeks before the explosion on 24th May 1901. He was then 30 years of age but already had experience as a fireman, overman and under-manager.

In the mine both Four Feet and Six Feet Seams were worked by what was known as the 'longwall' method. Under this system colliers, in each district being worked, were allocated a length of the coal face which they were responsible for excavating. The length — normally 11 yards at Senghenydd — was known as a particular collier's 'stall.' Thus, colliers in their individual stalls dug away the coal from the seam ahead of them and cut their way into it in a line-abreast formation like an army advancing on a broad front.

(It was a system which encouraged experienced colliers to bring in their young sons to work beside them as colliery boys. In time the boys, when they grew up, became colliers in their own right and passed their knowledge on to their own sons. But it was a practice which had its drawbacks — as Senghenydd was to learn — inasmuch as in a major disaster father and son perished together).

As the colliers cut out the coal they used any resulting rocks and debris to support the roof behind them. This packing of debris was known as the goaf or, more usually in South Wales, the gob. Roadways 10 to 12 feet wide were maintained between the debris pillars in the gob to allow trams or waggons to be brought up to the face to take away the coal being cut. In these roadways the roof was also supported with vertical and horizontal props of timber. The roads were normally about 15 yards apart and at right angles to the open face. At their other end they connected with a branch of the main haulage system of the mine. In this way coal was hauled out and supplies brought in to the working colliers.

As the work on the face moved forward so pressure caused the roof to settle on to the debris in the gob behind the colliers. In fact, at Senghenydd, the debris pillars about 100 yards back from the face were often compressed into half their original bulk and even completely solidified. This gradual settling of the roof meant that the roads were also continually affected and their height diminished.

To preserve the height of these roads it was necessary to take down the roof or deepen the roadway itself. In either case the debris removed could be carried forward to the face to provide additional material for packing the support pillars or gob behind the colliers. Otherwise it would be hauled to the surface to add to the colliery tip. Where the roof stratum was soft the required height could be obtained by taking down the roof with picks and wedges, but in the Universal Colliery it was generally hard and this meant it had to be blasted out with explosives.

Blasting was normally carried out between the end of the day shift and the beginning of the night shift — that is between 5:00 and 6:30pm — but it was also allowed, if required, between the night and day shifts.

Edward Shaw — Manager and Agent of the Universal Colliery, Senghenydd *('Western Mail' photograph)*

By day 450 men and boys were employed below ground with 240 by night. The night shift finished work at 4:30am after which they made their way through the workings to pit bottom at the Lancaster shaft to await an ascent to home, a meal, sleep and safety.

Normally the walk to pit bottom took anything from minutes to half an hour. In the early hours of the morning of Friday, 24th May 1901 for eighty-one men in the pit this journey took a lifetime.

Chapter 4

Practice makes perfect

AS THE SOUND of Big Ben striking the last note of five o'clock on the morning of Friday, 24th May 1901 died away, the trumpeter on the parade square at Wellington Barracks pursed his lips to his trumpet and began to sound reveille. It was a call blown earlier than usual that morning and the guardsmen rousing to it realised only too well that it heralded a day ahead more than usually busy and exhausting. On the previous evening they had spent hours primping and combing busbies, cleaning and pipe-claying belts and rifle slings, polishing buttons and brass, and boning and polishing toe caps of boots to a mirror finish.

For weeks the chosen detachments of the Brigade of Guards had practised their formation drill, their marching and counter-marching in quick and slow time and rehearsed the whole intricate and precise procedure attending the ceremony of Trooping the Colour on the Horse Guards Parade. Today the practice and rehearsals of the past would accentuate the spectacle being made public when the King presented new colours to the 3rd Scots Guards and these colours were trooped before the assembled guards for their recognition. It was the anniversary of the birthday of Queen Victoria. Before she died in January that year it had been her intention to present new colours to the Scots Guards at this ceremony. Now her son, King Edward VII, was to carry out his mother's wishes.

As the trumpet notes shattered the sleep of the guards near Whitehall, far away on the Cote d'Azur in the South of France Sir William Thomas Lewis stirred uneasily in his sleep. He was taking a holiday in the Mediterranean for the benefit of his health.

In Senghenydd the night shift at the Universal Colliery had finished work and most of them had already left the pit and were on the surface on their way home. Three of the day shift firemen had already descended the pit to carry out their usual examination of the workings before the day shift men came in to work. Altogether, there were eighty-two men in the pit if one excluded the seven men already in one of the cages rapidly being drawn up to the surface. These were Daniel Lewis and John Davies of Commercial Street, David Morris of High Street, Daniel Lewis of Kingsley Place and Edward Watkins of Grove Terrace, all of Senghenydd. The other two, from Abertridwr, were Evan Jones and John Morgan, a night shift fireman.

As the cage neared the surface the seven men heard a growling rumble under their feet and this grew louder as the cage came to rest 'at bank.' Without speaking, but realising that danger roared up the shaft under their feet, they flung themselves out of the cage and dashed for the safety of the lamp room. The last to leave the cage was John Morgan the fireman. As he stepped out he felt the cage lift beneath him as it went careering upwards into the winding gear on a blasting, roaring exploding cloud of smoke and dust. The explosion blew apart the plank surface of the shaft throwing Morgan clear. Before he lapsed into unconsciousness he saw a similar cloud of smoke and dust erupt from the mouth of the York pit fifty yards away and heard the sound of a second explosion.

As they raced to the safety of the lamp room Morgan's companions from the cage heard the deafening boom of the two successive blasts and seconds later the terrifying sound of a third.

In London the trumpeter on the square in the Wellington Barracks finished his rousing call to all quarters, came smartly to attention and, with a guardsman's precision, marched back to the guardroom. He could not have known his reveille for the 3rd Scots Guards had been a Last Post for eighty-one men underground in a Welsh Valley.

In the South of France Sir William Thomas Lewis was still sleeping peace fully.

In Senghenydd the Universal Colliery had begun the rehearsal for a greater tragedy still twelve years ahead.

Chapter 5

Blood had no price in a wage agreement

Friday, 24th May 1901 — Day 1

Two explosions in quick succession, accompanied by the sound of splintering woodwork and tearing metal, stopped the home-going night shift men in their tracks as they made their way through Senghenydd. They turned instinctively towards the colliery to see the column of smoke and dust rising high above the winding gear of the York and Lancaster pits. As they watched, they heard the third explosion and felt the ground shudder under their feet.

As realisation dawned with all its attendant fear the word 'Explosion,' or 'Tanchwa' in Welsh, was whispered in awe or shouted in surprised horror on all sides. Men near home dashed to tell their families they were safe. Others turned to rush back to the colliery they had just left. These adjured their home-rushing friends or relations to "Tell our mam (or my wife) that I'm all right. I'm going back to see if I can help." Already a mining community's concern for its own was manifesting itself, little knowing that within seconds their ready help could benefit only one man and two horses among the eighty-two men and fifty-two horses burning, suffocating and being blasted into bloody fragments below them underground.

All over Senghenydd and Abertridwr lights appeared in houses as candles and lamps flickered into life and as miners, ambulancemen, policemen, doctors and their families, awakened by the thudding explosions, prepared to confirm their worst fears and to give what help they could. Soon the streets leading towards the colliery were thronged with running, hurrying men, women and children in various states of dress and undress but all intent on the still smoking maw of the two pits.

When the explosions happened Edward Shaw, the manager, was at home in bed, but in minutes he was at the pit-head assessing the available

The scene at the Universal Colliery after the explosion on 24th May 1901
(permission of the Illustrated London News Picture Library)

information and directing operations. His hurried check showed the explosions which had blasted off the coverings of the shafts had also damaged the headings or covers of the ventilating fan. However, the fan itself was not damaged and had kept working.

The immediate needs were threefold: to maintain ventilation in the pit; to determine the number and identity of the men still below ground and, thirdly, by examination, to decide whether the winding gear was fit to allow officials and others to descend the shafts to assess the damage underground. Then rescue parties could be sent in to explore the working places to bring out survivors or, at worst, the dead.

The covering to the fan was quickly repaired and clean air once more began to be drawn down the Lancaster shaft. Whilst this was being done the tally check at the lamp room indicated that at least seventy-eight men still had lamps booked out to them. Thus it was likely that this was the minimum number of men below ground and calling for rescue.

The examination of the winding gear showed that the cage, which weighed over three tons and had brought the last seven men up the pit, had careered upwards into the horizontal lattice girders of the head gear. There two of its safety gates had remained crushed against the head gear when the cage fell back to be held secure by the keps or catches at the surface. Shaw attempted to operate the cages in the Lancaster pit but this failed when he found that the cage which was down the pit could not be moved. He concluded that it was jammed or obstructed by debris and machinery blown into the shaft by the explosion and ordered the rope of that cage to be detached from the winding drum. Immediately this had been done Shaw led a shift of men down the shaft in the free cage. They failed to get to pit bottom in the cage due to obstruction, as Shaw had rightly envisaged, from trams blown into the shaft by the explosion. The cage, with Shaw and his party, came to rest about 18 feet from pit bottom and from that point volunteers shinned down the guide ropes to clear the obstruction. By ten o'clock the obstructing trams and debris had been removed and the cage could be lowered all the way. In the meantime news of the explosion had flashed around the coal field and by the time Shaw got back to the surface a body of mining experts had arrived to advise and assist him.

As soon as it was known the cage could be lowered unimpeded to pit bottom two parties of examiners and rescuers made the descent; one party to examine the east side of the colliery and the other the west side. These parties were headed by R. T. Rees, the agent to the Universal Colliery, and Edward Shaw, accompanied by J. Dyer Lewis, an Assistant Inspector of Mines, and a number of managers and officials of nearby collieries. They were augmented by further shifts of men who went down the pit at 11:30am.

As the first parties pushed their way into the workings on both east and west sides of the shafts those going into the west side found their way blocked by a massive fall of roof about 60 yards from pit bottom. On the east side the first great fall was met about 300 yards along the main roadway. In getting to it the rescuers, when they were about 55 yards in, came across what they thought was the body of William Harris, an ostler, lying by the side of his dead horse. Harris was severely burned about the head, face and hands and seemed unconscious. In fact his appearance led most of the party to believe he was dead, but as Doctor Burke, the Medical Officer to the Llanbradach Colliery, made to examine him, Harris moved his arm and groaned. The effect on the rescuers was electrifying and they were elated and heartened to find someone alive so soon in their exploration.

The excitement of discovering Harris alive with the hope it engendered in both the rescuers underground and the anxious, expectant crowds at the surface, was to be one of those quirks of fate often occurring so inexplicably in major calamities. It seemed designed to make ultimate despair even more desperate.

Harris was whisked up the pit, examined, cleaned and treated in the lamp room then taken to his home swathed in bandages. At the time there was little hope for his survival.

As the rescuers inched their way into the mine any elation at finding someone alive evaporated quickly. On the east side just beyond the main intake they found the bodies of John Jones, timberman, of 15 Kingsley Place and of Thomas Coombes, an assistant timberman, of High Street. On the west side, in the stable crossing, the other rescue party found the body of George Warren, an ostler of 44 Stanley Street. All three men were from Senghenydd and married: Jones had three children, Coombes had two and George Warren had six. The flicker of hope, sparked by finding Harris, died with the discovery of the three dead near the shaft. It implied little likelihood of others being alive further into the workings — or 'inbye' as miners referred to it. The final twist that day came when rescuers reached the stables on the east side and found two horses alive out of the four in the stable. The two alive were those nearest the blast from the explosion. With Harris they were to be the only living things to survive the disaster.

In the meantime J. T. Robson, H.M. Inspector of Mines, with his assistant, Mr Adams, had arrived at the colliery and begun their examination of the plans of the workings. When the parties of explorers came up the

William Harris — The sole survivor of the explosion on 24th May 1901 *(permission of his daughter, Mrs K. Moore)*

pit at 2pm Robson and Adams consulted with them and prepared to descend the pit to make their own examination. They were accompanied by Bruce Jones of Abercynon Collieries and J. H. Jones, Manager of Fochriw Colliery. What Robson and Adams saw confirmed all that the exploration parties had told them about the massive falls in the main haulage roads and how far they extended along the roads. Later Robson was to say, in his report, 'the falls were both higher and more continuous than I have seen after any explosion in South Wales or elsewhere.'

This was reaffirmed by one of the rescuers, who had also taken part in rescue operations after the disaster in 1894 at the Albion Colliery, Cilfynydd, near Pontypridd, when 290 men were killed. He told a 'Western Mail' reporter, "You can't compare this with the Albion. Here we found fall after fall of great length and covered with timber blown from all directions and for hundreds of yards. In many places the roof had been stripped of every piece of timber and trams had been carried by the force of the blast on to the top of the falls where some of them were wedged in between the roof and the fall."

Other indications of the extent and violence of the explosion, found as exploration proceeded, were that air doors and their frames had been torn from the brick walls supporting them. The doors had been blown to fragments, and the brick supports themselves had been shattered. Also amongst this evidence of the vicious destructive force of the explosion was the finding of one poor miner whose lamp had been embedded in his body by the blast. The rescue parties were to witness many such grisly scenes of charring and mutilation as they gradually came upon the bodies of miners who had felt the full force of the explosion and faced the heat and blast it engendered.

Thus, the worst fears of the exploring parties about the severity of the explosion were being confirmed each yard they advanced towards the coal faces on both east and west sides — the faces where they hoped, against receding hope, to find survivors.

On the west side they found the main return airway was, generally speaking, untouched by the explosion and this was read as enabling rescuers, subject to adequate ventilation, to probe into most of the faces on that side. It was an assumption which was later proved to be over-optimistic when massive falls were encountered blocking the way into the Mafeking and Pretoria Districts.

On the east side heavy falls obstructed both the intake and return roads. This implied a prolonged and sustained effort to overcome them, to restore ventilation and so reach survivors and bodies on that side of the pit

This problem of clearing a passage for men and ventilation over or through the falls was now of paramount importance and teams of twenty men, for each side of the pit, were organised to do this. Whilst rescue was still the prime motive it was already being recognised from the conditions being uncovered that there was little likelihood of anyone else being found alive. If confirmation of this was needed the train from Cardiff which drew into Senghenydd Station at 7:30pm on that evening brought it. It unloaded 40 coffins for delivery to the Universal Colliery.

The first official statement about the explosion, its extent and the action being taken with the Inspectors of Mines, was made late on Friday afternoon by William Thomas Rees, the managing director of the colliery company. In the meantime Sir William Thomas Lewis had been informed of the calamity and he immediately required that, until his return, he be provided with a progress report every four hours.

On the surface a crowd of thousands from all the nearby mining valleys had gathered and among them were the distraught parents, wives and relatives of the men underground and still unaccounted for. This sorry group were comforted by detachments of the Salvation Army drafted in from Cardiff and the surrounding valleys. With the police the Salvation Army lasses persuaded some of the worried families to return to their homes to await any news. Despite the promise by the police to despatch news by runners, many of them chose to stay near the pit-head, possibly in the forlorn hope and belief that their physical presence would in some way help those fathers, sons, husbands and brothers still underground.

Apart from those of Warren, Jones and Coombes no more bodies were brought up on that first day. Down below exploration was halted by the falls and work on these was frequently held up as concentrations of gas were encountered. Precious time was lost until these were dispersed and work could recommence. This work continued all through the night. As dawn broke crowds again began to gather around the pit-head in expectation of news from the tired men coming up the pit after working all night on the back-breaking work of clearance.

Saturday, 25th May 1901 — Day 2

On Saturday morning the official machinery to meet the legal needs attending sudden death began to move. At the Gwern y Milwr Hotel on the village square in Senghenydd, Mr E. B. Reece, the Coroner, formally opened the inquiry into the circumstances of the death of the three men whose bodies had been brought up on the previous day. Sixteen jurymen were sworn in and the Revd D. Roberts, the Minister of Salem Baptist

Chapel at Senghenydd was appointed as foreman. Also present to hold watching briefs were Ben Davies, Rhondda miners' agent; W. P. Nicholas, solicitor of Pontypridd, representing the Miners' Federation of Great Britain and Charles Goodfellow, a solicitor, representing some of the deceased's families. Evidence of identification of Warren, Jones and Coombes was given and the hearing was then adjourned until Monday.

At the home of William Lewis in Thomas Street, Abertridwr, that morning, a Post Office messenger tried to deliver a telegram addressed to Lewis informing him his wife had died of cancer at Cardiff Royal Infirmary during the night. Lewis was unable to receive it; he was somewhere in the East District in the colliery and rescuers had not yet reached him. A neighbour advised the telegraph boy to take the telegram to Lewis' sister, Mrs Anslow, living in High Street, Senghenydd. The news contained in the buff envelope was not entirely unexpected by Mrs Anslow; she knew of her sister-in-law's condition and when she had been taken into hospital had assumed the care of her brother's three children. The telegram meant that the responsibility she had assumed on a temporary basis was now to become permanent. With her own seven children, she was now to have a family of ten. Her husband, William Anslow, did not return from the Universal Colliery for another three days when he was brought home in his coffin on Tuesday afternoon.

The inquest hearing in the morning was followed in the afternoon and in the same hotel by a meeting of the members of the Executive Council of the South Wales Miners' Federation at which Mabon (William Abraham, MP for Rhondda) presided.

The meeting expressed its condolences with the families of the deceased and then moved on to decide what practical action the organisation could take to alleviate the suffering of dependants and to ensure the protection of their interests. The officials of the Federation were empowered to grant families £20 to £50 for funeral and other expenses. (This amount would be recoverable from the compensation ultimately payable to the families.) Finally they decided the executive members to represent the Federation at the adjourned inquest would be Ben Davies, Evan James, James Manning, George Barker, the Chairman (Mabon), the Vice-Chairman (William Brace), the Treasurer (Alfred Onions) and the Secretary (Tom Richards). These members were also required to form a relief fund committee to issue a public appeal.

For the crowds gathered around the pit-head these deliberations of the trade union and the Crown were of passing importance only. Their thoughts, hopes and anxieties were all concentrated below ground on the work of rescue, with the misery or jubilation likely to result from the heroic efforts being made there. Little did they know on that Saturday that the day's efforts, with those of Sunday, would serve only to unloose the flood of tears and sorrow then being restrained by a frail dam wall of anxious hopes.

Sunday, 26th May 1901 — Day 3

This dam was breached completely on Sunday when W. T. Rees, the managing director of the colliery company, issued two official statements — one at 2pm and the other at 8pm. These reported most of the working places on the east side had been explored and seven bodies, including that of the day fireman, John G. Evans, had been found. However the falls there were so heavy it had not yet been possible to bring out the bodies. On the other side of the pit in the Ladysmith District fifteen bodies had been found and several of them had been recovered. The main road to the Pretoria District in the south west was blocked by a massive fall and this had to be removed or overcome to reach the men known to have been working there.

Rees also went on to report that by noon on that Sunday fifteen bodies in all had been brought up with the others expected during the day. He confirmed good progress was being made towards entering the Kimberley District in the west; relays of men in several gangs were pushing ahead with exploration and the clearance of falls on all roads; air crossings had been restored so that in-going fresh air by-passed out-going foul air to ensure ventilation of the workings; winding was now possible with both cages and ventilation was passing into the mine through most of the falls. His later report told of progress in the attempt to get through the falls blocking the roads to both Pretoria and Kimberley Districts.

To the knowledgeable miners among the crowds of thousands surrounding the pit-head all through that day these two reports of massive falls in all districts of the mine were read as indicating no hope for survivors.

This reaction was reflected in the headlines of local and national newspapers the following day when they announced all hope for survivors had been abandoned. The official statements had said nothing about the prospect of finding survivors but those who live with danger are quick to read the signs. The two villages in the valley knew on that day that the prospect now facing them was one of burying their dead if and when they were found and a long bleak future without the presence and support of their menfolk.

For Mrs Anslow it was confirmation she now had ten children to care for without her husband or her brother to provide for them.

The bodies being recovered were all sickeningly mutilated, disfigured and burned. The ambulancemen, mortuary attendants and doctors did yeoman work to ensure their cleanliness and presentability for identification before they were placed in their coffins and carried home on the shoulders of their workmates and neighbours. In very many cases identification depended entirely on personal trivia like belt buckles, metal buttons, pocket watches, tins for 'twists' of tobacco, and such like.

Many of the families were never to see the bodies of their menfolk. Due to the state of the bodies they were advised to bury the coffins unopened. Some coffins contained little of the remains of the men who had gone to work on the previous Thursday night. What little had been found was made up to bodyweight by weights wrapped into the winding sheet.

Out of respect for the feelings for the bereaved families and for the stricken community as a whole, the dead were borne to their homes after dark; carried shoulder high by friends in a quiet lamplit procession through the hushed streets of the two villages.

At those homes the lasses of the Salvation Army, with their apposite motto of 'Blood and Fire,' provided a woman's care and comfort for the sorrowing womenfolk, children and relations. They took charge of running homes, cooking meals, acting as foster mothers in caring for children and provided solace for women broken under the weight of their grief.

Monday, 27th May 1901 — Day 4

Next morning the resumed inquest took evidence of identification of the thirty-three bodies recovered by then. Coroner Reece was moved to comment the bodies they had viewed were really not in a fit state to be seen and ought to be buried at once. Also, on the recommendation of Doctor James of Senghenydd, he decided that in the best interests of health no more bodies would be viewed by the jury; this was comment enough on the effects of explosion and fire on flesh and blood. He then adjourned the inquest until 17th June, by which time he expected the report of J. T. Robson, Chief Inspector of Mines, to be available.

Around the colliery the weekend crowd of thousands had dwindled to hundreds. This was a silent and visual acknowledgement by the inhabitants of the coal field that hope had vanished. From now on they could not properly intrude on the grief and distress flowing from ultimate confirmation of death. It was now the very private concern of Senghenydd and Abertridwr.

Below ground the rescue teams and helpers from the colliery itself had been augmented and reinforced by the experience and technical know-how of managers, officials, colliers, repairers and all types of workmen from collieries as diverse as the Lady Windsor, Ynysybwl; the Ocean-Treharris Colliery; Cymmer Colliery at Porth; the Great Western at Pontypridd; Nixon's Colliery; Mountain Ash; National Colliery, Wattstown; Clydach Vale Colliery; Dowlais Collieries; Llanbradach Colliery; and from the Bertie Pit, the Tower Pit and Havod Pit of the Lewis-Merthyr Collieries. The effort being put into exploration and rescue was undoubtedly immense, sustained and valiant.

The official statement issued at 5pm on Monday reported good progress on the east side with an improvement in ventilation there. On the west side teams of workers had broken a way through the fall reported on Sunday as blocking their way into the Pretoria District only to find another mammoth fall about 60 to 70 feet high before them. The parties trying to push their way into the Kimberley and Mafeking Districts had got through an immense fall on the double parting into these districts and then found another large fall ahead of them.

(A 'double parting' was an arrangement in the system for the haulage of laden and unladen trams. It was a parallel loop of tramrails enabling outgoing laden trams to pass incoming empty trams. One journey of trams remained stationary on its own line whilst the other journey passed.)

The main task of the working parties was still that of making a way into all the working places in the pit in case there were still some men, even one man, left alive in a remote corner. To make any progress at all it was of paramount importance to restore and improve ventilation — without it the falls blocking the way could not be tackled. As it was it was physically impossible for falls to be cleared immediately; it was a case of going over, around, under or through by the quickest and safest way. This usually meant going over the fall by opening up a passageway through which air and men could safely and continuously find a way. Any bodies buried by the falls and not uncovered in the process of breaking through had to be left to be discovered when work on clearing the falls completely could be started.

By midnight on Monday a total of forty-seven bodies had been brought to the surface, with those recovered during the day being found in the York East and the No 2 South Districts.

At his home William Harris was in a pitiable state but still alive and, although often delirious, had made some progress. He was being tended by Nurse Wiseman from Cardiff and was still dangerously ill. Nevertheless hope was growing for his recovery.

Tuesday, 28th May 1901 — Day 5

As Tuesday dawned the attention of the world, through its representatives the newspaper reporters, was drawn away from the colliery and fleetingly directed at the wounds inflicted on families, friends, neighbours and acquaintances in a small, tightly knit community when they perform the mournful ritual of burying their dead.

Before six o'clock on that May morning families in five houses were awake and about. Breakfast for many of them was no more than a cup of tea; they were, as the Welsh say, 'full up' with grief and would have gagged on solid foods. Their houses had been cleaned to a shining spotlessness and fires burned merrily in the lustrous black-leaded facia of their grates. Chairs had been assembled to seat the relatives and friends expected to arrive before 8am. In some of the houses the family Bible had been placed in the centre of the chenille cloth covering the table. Today another death would be entered on the Bible's flyleaf where the family's births, marriages and deaths were faithfully recorded. Before eight o'clock male friends, workmates and neighbours were gathering outside each of the five houses. There they clustered in hushed conversation in small groups, all self conscious in navy blue or black serge suits, bowler hats, stiffly starched white collars, black ties and well polished boots. Horse drawn hearses, their glass sides and silver fittings sparkling in the morning sunshine, with their black horses, replete in their black trappings and nodding plumes, stood ready outside three of the houses. Outside the others sombre black biers had been placed.

As eight o'clock approached a clergyman entered each house to offer sympathy and solace to the widows, parents and children and to hold a short service before the dead miner left his home for the last time. At the home of George Filer in High Street the Salvation Army conducted the service.

When the short services in the houses were over the coffins of the dead were carried out and placed in the hearses or on the biers. The men waiting in the street outside doffed their hats and stood in respectful silence as this was done. In the Welsh fashion before a funeral 'rises' or moves off those attending the funeral sing a hymn, as only Welsh voices can sing. This morning there were no hymns. Instead the waiting men quietly moved to take up their places, in twos, before the hearses or the biers. The mourning relations formed up behind the coffins and the appointed bearers lifted the biers on to their shoulders. At a signal the individual processions moved off and made their slow and sorrowful way through Senghenydd. In all the houses in the village blinds and curtains were drawn and tight-lipped men and women, some quietly sobbing, stood by the doors of their houses or lined the streets to pay their silent last respects to the dead.

In the processions where the coffins were carried on biers four men rhythmically dropped out of the main body every hundred yards or so and stood silently, two on each side of the procession which passed between them. As the bier arrived where they stood they moved, one to each handle, to take over the bier from the bearers. These bearers then resumed their place in the procession ready, if required, to shoulder their burden further along the route. This was a visible sharing of the burden of sorrow and a mining village's last mark of respect to its own.

Like five black caterpillars the processions wove their way through Senghenydd to the square at its centre where they joined to climb the slight rise to the railway station. There on the 8:30am train the dust of four men took train to return to their native dust – George Griffith of Commercial Street to return to Llanelli; John Harvey of Stanley Street to Newport, Mon; John Davies of Commercial Street to Newcastle Emlyn and that of James James of Caerphilly Road to Newport, Pembrokeshire. George Filer's body left for Treorchy on the 9:30am train.

In the early afternoon an open hearse took the body of William Thomas Evans, a single man, to Newbridge. Later that afternoon a mass funeral for six Senghenydd men — George Warren of 44 Stanley Street; Thomas Coombes of 26 High Street; Edward Bennett and William James of Caerphilly Road; and George Griffiths and Llewellyn Llewellyn of Parc Terrace — wended its three mile way to the little churchyard of Eglwysilan set in a fold of the mountain above Abertridwr. Once again the funerals were marked by the absence of singing. Instead, there was the moving, silent and solemn respect of a mining community which stood bareheaded to watch them pass. There is a belief in Wales that its countrymen sing best in sorrow, rather than in elation, but this was one sorry occasion when hearts were too full to sing. Twelve men from Senghenydd were buried in their native soil on this Tuesday setting the pattern for more mass funerals in the coming weeks — and twelve years later.

Far below the graves gouged out of the hillside at Eglwysilan working parties were concentrating on breaking through into the three remaining unexplored districts of Pretoria, Mafeking and Kimberley on the west side of the colliery workings. Other parties were consolidating airways and roadways behind the exploration parties and removing falls already overcome or circumvented. The day's efforts resulted in four more bodies being found bringing the number recovered up to fifty-one.

Ventilation was still top priority below ground and even where it was restored it was not improved by the ever present smells of gas, charred timbers and brattice, coked coal dust and the strange sickly stench of burnt decomposing flesh of both men and horses. The bodies of some of the rotting horses were disposed of during the day by a team of horse slaughterers, assisted by working parties of miners. These cut up the bodies into manageable pieces to bury in quick lime in the workings underground. Little imagination is needed to envisage the job these men did; a newspaper report described the horses as being 'in a bad state of decomposition' and grossly understated their disposal as 'an unpleasant duty.'

The push towards the Pretoria District during the day was halted by concentrations of gas which the inadequate ventilation failed to disperse. To overcome this Shaw and his advisers decided to enlarge the way over the mountainous falls encountered the previous day and, where possible, to increase the size of all air courses and crossings. The theory was that this would enable a current of air to be diverted towards the falls blocking the way into the remaining unexplored districts and literally force air over them to dilute or disperse the concentrations of gas accumulating behind them. Until this was done progress in breaching an entrance into both Mafeking and Pretoria would be halted. Shaw and his counsellors agreed that Mafeking should be tackled first and Pretoria afterwards.

In the meantime a call had gone around the coal field for horses and harnesses and these arrived this Tuesday. They replaced those horses killed in the explosion and provided the power for moving trams of debris removed from falls to clear roadways and airways more quickly.

Wednesday, 29th May 1901 — Day 6

The policy of concentrating on ventilating an unexplored district by forcing fresh air over the falls of rock blocking entry into the district began to pay dividends quickly. By Wednesday a way into Mafeking had been secured, the working places had been explored and, by the end of the day, five bodies had been brought out.

That afternoon the streets of the two mining villages were again respectfully solemn and silent as those living there watched the coffins of eleven of their men journey to the churchyard at Eglwysilan and two to the graveyard of the chapel at Groeswen.

Thursday, 30th May 1901 — Day 7

The toll of bodies recovered increased to sixty-five on Thursday when six more were brought out of the Mafeking workings and three from other parts of the mine. The progress with exploration and clearance evinced the official forecast during the day that the pit was likely to be reopened for work in six or seven weeks.

Nevertheless the falls blocking the way into Pretoria had still to be overcome and this was the last major exploratory task left before the back breaking job of restoration and reconstruction could begin in earnest. With Pretoria explored it was expected most of the dead would be accounted for leaving only isolated bodies to be retrieved as falls were cleared. Only then could the rehabilitation and reconstruction of the mine to restore normal working be tackled as a whole, with all its implications of clearance, consolidation and repair or replacement of machinery and plant. By now men rendered idle by the explosion had been out of work for a week and some were moved to consider seeking work at nearby collieries over the coming weekend. The colliery company appreciated the possibility of this loss of their workforce and considered arrangements for any men not engaged on exploration and clearance to be employed in other Lewis-Merthyr pits. Even so, many of the men heeded the warning provided by an explosion which had swept through all the workings. They left never to return to the Universal. Others who did not return were the seven men buried on Thursday and the eleven on Friday.

Friday and Saturday, 31st May and 1st June 1901 — Days 8 & 9

Following the breakthrough into Mafeking, Edward Shaw now concentrated on ventilating the Pretoria District to effect entry there. This took all day on Friday, but by Saturday a way in had been secured. In the faces on the north side of the ingress eight bodies were found and brought out, but the faces to the south could not be explored that day due to the heavy concentrations of gas confronting the explorers.

In the afternoon the two horses — called Tenby and Radnor — which had survived the explosion were brought out of the pit. An earlier attempt to bring them up singly on the Friday had to be abandoned when they stubbornly refused to be separated. The equine 'comrades-in-arms' were brought out together on Saturday and, according to an eye witness, both of them trotted sprightly out of the cage at the surface on their way to the stables and appeared no worse for their experience.

By the evening of Saturday the repair to the lip of the York pit had been completed and it was then able to be used for raising, in specially constructed buckets, the water which was seeping into and collecting in parts of the workings.

Sunday, 2nd June 1901 — Day 10

Sunday saw the suspension of all work in the pit. The worst was known and recognised so clearance of the roads and workings and the recovery of the remaining eight bodies, wherever they might be lying undetected, could wait for twenty-four hours. As it was the bodies being recovered after lying for ten days in the foetid atmosphere in the faces called for immediate burial. This is borne out by the report that the bodies of Andrew Diegan, a young Irishman lodging in High Street, Senghenydd, with that of William Jenkin Jones of Commercial Street, were both buried on Sunday within hours of being brought out of Pretoria on Saturday. Burial on a Sunday was exceptional and this indicates the extreme state of decomposition of the bodies then being found.

Monday, 3rd June 1901 — Day 11 — and later

When work was resumed the next day two bodies were recovered from under the fall blocking the way into Pretoria and one from a fall near the North Stables, bringing the toll of those recovered to seventy-six.

From here on the discovery of more bodies was sporadic. Of the five still to be recovered the body of Ebenezer Davies was found on Friday, 7th June and that of Christopher Martin on the following Sunday. Martin's remains were identifiable only by his tobacco box and his time sheet.

The bodies of Gwilym Jones, David Davies and William Parker were still unrecovered over six weeks later when the adjourned inquest was reconvened.

By now the first Senghenydd explosion had ceased to be news and by the first week in June the world had lost interest. News of the war against the Boers in South Africa had resumed its former pride of place and its casualty lists were more newsworthy than the effect on a South Wales valley of the death of eighty-one miners.

At the colliery over 120 men were still working day and night to clear the falls and to restore the mine to working order; others had found work elsewhere or were waiting for the mine to reopen for normal working.

William Harris had recovered physically but was grievously disfigured on hands and head by burns and was mentally confused. He was firmly convinced he alone had sustained an accident underground and that no other men had been involved.

But in other homes in the valley parents, widows and fatherless children knew to their cost that others were involved. For all these their involvement would continue and the effects would have to be endured for many a hard year ahead.

Mrs. Anslow had her new family of ten to provide and care for. The widow of John Thomas of Stanley Street, Senghenydd, had five children between the age of 4 and 10 years to bring up and Mrs Jacob Lewis of 'The Huts,' who had lost both her husband and her 21 year old son, had seven children to mother.

Their dead menfolk had become mere additional numbers lost in the total of over 1,830 miners killed in disasters in Welsh mines from December 1875 — when the first sliding scale wage agreement was ratified — to May 1901.

By the same token the three widows and their children became similar statistics among the valley's 57 widows and 230 fatherless children created by the first explosion at Senghenydd. In turn these hundreds merged into the massive total of over 5,000 dependants left destitute by mining disasters in Wales since the inception of the wages agreement. For all these women and children the selling price of coal held no importance; they were already aware of some of the cost of winning it. The remainder of the cost would be paid in poverty, grief and suffering over the years. What the full extent of these would be was a question no-one was, or is, capable of answering.

In the meantime other questions were calling for immediate answer.

Chapter 6

Questions and Answers — with lessons for the learning

ON 1st JUNE 1901 the Home Secretary, C. T. Ritchie MP, asked Professor W. Galloway, the Professor of Mining at the University College of South Wales and Monmouthshire, to provide a report on the circumstances attending the explosion.

He was the son of William Galloway, JP, a Paisley coal owner, and the brother of Robert Lindsay Galloway, doyen of coal mining historians. Galloway, eventually knighted for his services to coal mining, resigned an appointment as Inspector of Mines prior to accepting the chair of mining in South Wales, so his experience, observations and conclusions were invaluable in determining what had happened and what ought to be done to prevent a recurrence. His report was completed and submitted to the Home Secretary on 15th July 1901.

This was in time for its consideration at the inquest hearing set for 22nd July 1901 following its further adjournment from 17th June. However, when that Monday morning arrived the bodies of Gwilym Jones, David Davies and William Parker had still not been found. Because Jones and Davies were thought to have cartridges and firing apparatus in their possession Coroner E. Bernard Reece felt that the absence or presence of these items on the bodies was material evidence on which could hinge a conclusion where the explosion had originated. Thus, Galloway's report was held in abeyance when the Coroner decided to adjourn the inquest until Monday, 21st October 1901. By that time he expected these three remaining bodies would be found and all the necessary evidence would be available to enable the questions engaging every interested person to be answered.

These all-important questions called for an examination of the past and current practices in the working of the Universal Colliery, with conclusive decisions on why the explosion happened, how and where it happened and whether anyone should have to account for acts of omission or commission causing the disaster. Finally, were there lessons to be learned from the disaster which could be applied to the industry as a whole to prevent a recurrence?

Galloway's report to the Home Secretary was decisive on the answers to most of these questions and there is little doubt that if the message it contained had been heeded the second Senghenydd explosion in 1913 could well have been avoided

The report clearly identified all the factors affecting the conditions favouring an explosion and the relative importance of each of these in such a situation; these concerned the presence of gas, air, coal dust, water and the deadly igniting spark or flame. To appreciate Galloway's contentions in full one needs to be apprised of the change in thinking, concerning the main cause of colliery explosions, which had slowly been gaining credence between 1800 and 1901. This related to the part played by coal dust in explosions.

In the early 1800s the cause of explosions began to attract scientific attention and the accepted premise was that the explosive element in coal mines was methane, or firedamp as the miners called it.

Coal, as a mineral fuel, had been formed by the decomposition of vegetable matter and its subsequent compression by overlays of further vegetable matter, silt, soil and rocks. Methane, or marsh gas, was generated in the process of decay and bubbles, and even large pockets of it, were trapped in the vegetable matter stratum in the compression process. When a coal seam was worked the gas was released in small emissions all along a face and, on the basis of 'many a mickle makes a muckle,' could result in the concentration of gas reaching explosive proportions. Where a large pocket of gas escaped this was known to miners as a 'blower.' Some of these blowers were so large that, by 1901, cases had been recorded in the South Wales coal field of miners being suffocated by them.

The need to prevent unguarded flames igniting the gas in coal mines and preventing the usual attendant explosion led to the invention of the Davy lamp in 1815. This was a major step forward in the search for increased safety in mines. However, major explosions continued to occur and when Faraday and Lyell reported on the disaster at the Haswell Colliery in Northumberland in 1844, when ninety-five men were killed, their opinion was that coal dust had provided fuel to the flame of what was considered to be a firedamp explosion. Nevertheless, the theory still persisted that firedamp was the essential element of every colliery explosion with coal dust being only a contributory or aggravating ingredient.

These views continued to have credence into the 1870s and 1880s when Galloway reported to the Royal Society. Following his investigations into explosions in dry and dusty mines, he had concluded — and proved these conclusions by experiment — that fine coal dust mixed with air formed an explosive mixture. His experiments had proved a coal dust and air mixture exploded without any firedamp being present. Furthermore, he showed that once the mixture was ignited the air disturbance it caused raised further coal dust to perpetuate the explosive and burning processes.

He felt that a coal dust explosion could originate in the disturbance and flame produced by a small local explosion of firedamp or by a blasting shot, whether a normal shot or 'blown out' shot.

The term 'blown out shot' calls for explanation. The operation of blasting, as practised in the Universal and other collieries, involved boring a hole from two to four feet deep by 1¼ to 1½ inches in diameter in the ground above or below the coal seam. This hole was charged with explosive and tamped in, or plugged, firmly with clay or other material. The charge was then fired by a fuse or electric battery. Normally the ground would be broken up by the exploding charge and the shot hole destroyed in the process. If, however, the ground resisted the charge to a greater degree than the tamping in the drill hole, the tamping would be blown out — as from a gun barrel — leaving the hole practically intact. Hence the term 'blown out shot.'

Galloway went on to say most colliery explosions originated with blasting shots, whether ordinary or blown out, and it had been shown 'that shots charged with ordinary blasting powder . . . produce a longer flame, and thus more readily raise and ignite coal dust, than those charged with nitroglycerine or nitrate of ammonia type . . .. It is, further, apparent that if a mine is made damp or wet artificially, coal dust explosions cannot occur in it whatever kind of explosive is used.'

If the message about dampness contained in that last sentence had been recognised and assiduously applied the lives of thousands of miners in Britain would not have continued to be put at risk and the name of Senghenydd would not have become synonymous with disaster. As it was, the Home Office had for some time made it compulsory to lay the coal dust in a naturally dry and dusty mine by watering roads, roof and sides for a radius of 20 yards around a shot hole before the shot was fired. Many mines, including the Universal, took this further and dampened the coal dust in haulage roads by water piped into the mine and used casks to water areas into which the pipes did not extend. This was not compulsory but it indicated a growing recognition of the danger of coal dust preached by Galloway.

He also demonstrated how appropriate the description 'dry and dusty mine' was to the Universal Colliery. By readings taken above and below the ground he showed that the temperature in the workings was about 25°F higher than at the surface due to the depth of the pit. This meant that the warmer air circulating through the workings absorbed the underground moisture making the mine dry — and, consequently, dusty. In fact his physical examination of the workings led him to say that the mine was dry and dusty when the explosion occurred.

Other factors he identified as aggravating the amount of coal dust in the mine, were the type of waggons used for transporting coal underground and the method of loading coal in these waggons.

The waggons were rectangular in shape and constructed of sheet iron enclosing three sides of the rectangle. The fourth side — one end of the waggon — was open except for two iron bars. These were hinged at one side and held by a pin and cotter to the other side to prevent large pieces of coal from falling on to the road.

It was the practice to load over a ton of coal in each waggon — and this meant the coal had to be built high — or 'raced' as the miners called it — above the sides and ends of the waggon. Inevitably some fell from the waggons in their journey to the surface and this coal was crushed underfoot into fine dust by horses and men. This dust covered the roadways and coated their roofs and sides, providing a continuous and explosive fuse trail from the shaft to all the working places at the coal faces. Galloway ended this part of his report with the pointed sentence '. . . this train of coal dust has been the means of carrying the explosion into practically every working place in the colliery.'

This conclusion was based on his examination of all roadways and working places in the mine. Evidence that the explosion had passed through any part of the colliery was to be seen in the overlay of coked coal dust left on timber and coal; the scorching, blackening and burning of timber and brattice; and in the roof falls and the upheaval of trams, waggons, machinery and timber.

These signs also indicated the direction in which the explosion had travelled through the mine; crusts of coked coal dust were found on one side of timbers whereas the other side was soft and velvety to the touch, indicating a fine mixture of dust and soot. The coked deposit showed the direction from which the explosion came, inasmuch as molten coal dust was blasted against the face of the timber, etc, as the explosion passed, with dust and soot settling on the surface shielded from the blast.

On this basis he deduced the explosion had passed from the east side to the west side traversing hundreds of yards of intake roadways whilst leaving the parallel return roadways virtually intact. This was due to the fact that the intake airways — used for hauling coal — were heavily contaminated with the dust falling from overloaded waggons. In the return airways the dust was inert stone dust – providing confirmation of Galloway's contention that coal dust and air was the explosive mixture which had flashed its deadly way into all the faces of the Universal Colliery.

The only parts not affected were those, like the return roads, where there was little coal dust or where it was naturally damp and this had laid the coal dust.

Where dust was systematically dampened in some mines, the methods used — and recommended by Galloway — were: spraying from water tanks hauled along the mine railways; spraying from water pipes laid down the shaft and along the roadways to feed valves for hoses and sprays (these first two systems were used in the Universal); and the injection of steam into the intake air, but this had the effect also of making working conditions hot and uncomfortable.

All these methods had proved effective to different degrees and Galloway instanced how, at Pochin Colliery, Tredegar, an explosion was halted by dampness caused by leakage from barrels transporting water out of the pit. At Llwynypia, Rhondda, he failed to find any dry coal dust on the sides and roof of a road over 500 yards long where only the floor was watered by a water tank.

To eliminate spillage from overfilled trams he advocated the use of dust-tight waggons filled only to the upper edges of their sides.

These recommendations for watering and waggons were destined to become law before the next explosion in the Universal Colliery and, in part, it was lax attention to these legal requirements that seared the name of Senghenydd into the annals of mining disasters.

Turning to the cause and source of the explosion, his opinion was that it had originated in the main road, called Dallimore's Level, into the East District and was caused by a blasting shot. He had found an empty shot hole in the roof and, not far away, a piece of crimped newspaper which 'looked as if it had been crushed into a narrow space and beaten with a mallet.' The ground around the hole was loose, as if the shot had been fired but not done all the work intended for it. He decided the paper had been used as tamping for a shot prepared by Thomas and Joseph Fullerlove, father and son, and blown out when the shot was fired. The bodies of the two men were found 100 yards away and Galloway envisaged they had retired to this spot to escape the effects of the shot and to prevent other men approaching the shot hole. These signs, coupled with indications of the direction of blast, led him to conclude that this was the site of the explosion.

Among the objections raised to this theory was one that the Fullerloves were not authorised shot firers and were most unlikely to have used their own fuse and explosive. (Later it was shown that laxity in the control of explosives could have allowed the Fullerloves to have drawn explosives and fired this shot.)

Whilst his speculations concerning the site of origin and cause of the explosion were to be contested at the adjourned inquest, no-one disagreed with his explanation how it traversed the whole mine. Galloway wrote:-

> The extension of the explosion from this, or any other point in the mine at which it originated is easily explained.
> A considerable volume of flame having been formed, a sudden expansion of the air took place, creating an airwave which swept through the roadways in every direction, raising the coal dust and mixing it with the air as it passed. The flame followed closely behind the airwave, rapidly increasing the volume of heated air and, consequently, the pressure that was driving it forward from behind.
> The airwave sent off a shoot into each roadway as it passed, and if the shoot found a sufficient supply of coal dust to sustain the flame, it became self supporting but, otherwise, it quickly died out.
> In this manner the whole of the workings that contained coal dust were rapidly traversed, and the explosion became an accomplished fact.

This was the gist of Professor Galloway's exhaustive report which was available to the Coroner and his jury when they reconvened at 10:30am on Trafalgar Day, 21st October 1901, in the Miners' Lodge room of the Gwern y Milwr Hotel in Senghenydd.

All the various interests were well represented and no expense had been spared to ensure that those interests were entrusted to the best 'silk' money could buy. For the colliery owners and their officials, B. Francis-Williams KC and Trevor Lewis had been briefed; Abel Thomas KC MP for the Miners' Federation of Great Britain; and the Home Office had instructed S. T. Evans KC MP. Professor Galloway and the four Inspectors of Mines, J. T. Robson, Mr Gray, J. Dyer Lewis and F. Adams were also present. Among the many local and national officers of the Miners' Federation were William Brace and D. Watts Morgan. The Officers of the

Court were Police Inspector Davies of Caerphilly and Sergeant Leyshon Williams of Senghenydd.

Whilst the Home Secretary would have Galloway's report and the official record of the inquest, he had also required reports from S. T. Evans KC and J. T. Robson, Inspector of Mines. All were destined to be unanimous on the danger of coal dust and the needs to counteract this by efficient watering.

The inquest opened with a formal identification by Griffith D. Griffiths of the bodies of Gwilym Jones and David Davies, recovered since the adjournment on 22nd July. It then moved on to establish the cause and origin of the explosion.

The evidence of the colliery agent, Robert T. Rees, the manager Edward Shaw, and many of the lower officials was so markedly similar it seemed that they worked in a different mine from that featuring in Galloway's report. According to them the ventilation was good; the roads were well watered from the pipes laid into the mine for that purpose, with casks being used elsewhere; that there was very little dust in the roads, but any found was cleared and sent to the surface each night. Rees contended several of the roads were naturally damp and the colliery as a whole was unusually wet for a steam coal mine. Both he and Shaw thought the explosion originated in the Pretoria District and had been caused by shot firing. Later evidence confirmed shots were due to be fired, between 5 and 6:30am that morning, in Pretoria to 'make height' for horses and trams in a heading into the district.

Also Rees and Shaw both believed that dust had carried the fire and explosion through the pit. This posed a question never put during the hearing; it concerned the inconsistency apparent in the theory of an explosion perpetuated by coal dust throughout a colliery so dust-free and well watered as described by these officials.

The next day's evidence swelled the chorus of little dust and assiduous watering — so much so, that by the end of the day, the jury must have felt, like the Queen in 'Hamlet,' that the witnesses 'doth protest too much, methinks.'

However, there were some surprising admissions also.

When describing the preparation for shot firing William Thomas, an overman, said that one cask of water was sufficient to dampen the defined area around where a shot was to be fired. (In a dry and dusty mine the Coal Mines Regulation Act required, it may be recalled, all places 'within a radius of 20 yards' from a shot hole to be 'in a wet state from thorough watering . . .') Also, he admitted, he never supervised the watering operation but always instructed the shot firer to do this properly. (With one cask of water?).

Thomas Morgan, the shot firer for the East District, confirmed watering was 'done properly' but he was under the impression he needed to water only for 20 yards along the roadway — not for a radius of the same measurement. His watering preparations had never been watched or supervised by manager, overmen or firemen. Finally he felt the wad of paper found in Dallimore Level was not part of a plug for a shot hole but was the wrapping off someone's dinner. It had probably been rolled up and compressed by a weight — a piece of rock — being placed upon it.

Nevertheless by far the most damning evidence heard that day was given by David Griffiths, the person appointed to have charge of explosives and detonators at the colliery.

The regulations then covering the control of these items were those in the Coal Mines Regulation Act, in the Explosives in Coal Mines Order of 24th September 1900 and in the Special Rules applied to steam collieries in the area.

These required strict control over the issue of detonators and explosives inasmuch as they were to be issued only to shot firers specially authorised by the owner, agent or manager in writing.

David Griffiths' evidence revealed that this was ignored at Senghenydd. He was in charge of the mine's stock of gelignite and detonators, with the main stock being held at the surface and a quantity kept in a small locked magazine underground. Whilst he had a key to this so did all the shotfirers, but he did not know who these were or how many there were. He kept no records of the amount taken from the surface magazine or of that taken from the store underground. Obviously, the lack of control over the issue of these items meant that shots were liable to be taken and fired by anyone capable of doing so. (This gave weight to Galloway's supposition that the Fullerloves could have done this).

When J. T. Robson, Inspector of Mines, was called to give evidence on the next day he answered a question, put by S. T. Evans KC on this control, by asserting that he would require one man to be responsible for issuing explosives. That man should know who had been nominated as shotfirers, and the quantity of the issue to any of those men should be recorded.

Other witnesses heard on that third day included Thomas Griffiths of Cymmer Colliery, Professor Galloway, two Assistant Inspectors of Mines — John Dyer Lewis and Mr Gray — and Thomas John, a collier.

As an employee, Thomas John stood out as the one person to strike a discordant note about dust. He had always seen plenty of dust on the roads, especially in the Pretoria District. It was particularly noticeable when a number of men were walking together along the roads. (One wonders whether he was subsequently blacklisted for employment in the coal field for this testimony.)

Thomas Griffiths of Cymmer Colliery and the three Mines Inspectors — Robson, Gray and Dyer Lewis — all felt the explosion originated on the west side and spread to the east side. Griffiths felt that a fall in the No 2 South had released a large quantity of gas and this had been ignited by the fireman's lamp on his way into the district.

The three Mines Inspectors were not unanimous about the point of origin on the west side although Robson and Dyer Lewis were both agreed it was somewhere in or near the No 2 South main road. (As in Pretoria, shot firing was scheduled to take place in No 2 South that morning so it is understandable that the district was suspect as the source of the explosion on this account.)

Gray, on the other hand, favoured the theory that the explosion started in the Pretoria District, and went on to say that, if the main roads running into Ladysmith and No 2 South districts had been sufficiently watered the explosion would have been confined to Pretoria and part of No 2 South. In that case the death toll would have been seventeen only, and the lives of the other sixty-four men who perished would have been saved. He further criticised management for not extending the water pipes into every district in the mine during the twelve months before the explosion. These extensions varied between 200 yards and 500 yards for individual districts.

Galloway's evidence reiterated all he had already said in his report and reaffirmed his contention that the explosion started on the east side. Replying to a question about this he said, "There is no question, this was a coal dust explosion caused by a shot fired in the East District in Dallimore's Level, which was too low for an ordinary horse." (This implied the shot was intended to bring down some roof to increase the height of the road.)

His answer to one other question is worth recording. When asked whether he thought the roads were sufficiently watered in the colliery, he said, "I am perfectly certain that on the morning of the explosion the roads were not sufficiently watered, otherwise the explosion would not have extended as it did."

The final bit of evidence was provided on the following day when the Coroner recalled Mines Inspector, J. T. Robson, to give an opinion why William Harris had not been killed with the other eighty-one men.

Robson said Harris had been rescued from a spot in the direct path of the blast from an explosion in Dallimore's Level. However, if the blast came from the west side some of the force would have escaped up the shafts. This strengthened his belief that the explosion originated on the west side.

Armed with this final piece of information the Coroner began his summing up by pointing out that the evidence and opinions presented at the hearing made it extremely difficult to determine the origin of the explosion. Even so, all the expert opinions agreed that the effects of the explosion had been carried by coal dust to all parts of the mine. Furthermore, the only way of preventing these extensive effects was by thorough and continuous watering of all roadways, with particular regard to the fact that the dust on the sides and roof of roadways was most dangerous.

He appreciated that currently there was no statutory obligation on mine owners to keep roadways watered in this way, but he took due note that Mr Robson, Mines Inspector, advocated stringent regulations be introduced to ensure this was done.

If, in arriving at their verdict, the jury could not decide where and how the explosion originated, it would be sufficient for them to find that the victims' deaths were caused by explosion in the Universal Colliery. Also, if they agreed with the Inspector's recommendations regarding watering to lay dust, they were free to consider whether they should add a rider to their verdict recommending that statutory provision should be made to make this compulsory.

Finally, the jury were required to note that all the Inspectors felt the manner of issuing explosives and detonators at the colliery was decidedly lax and they could consider whether to make a recommendation to the colliery owners concerning this.

The jury then withdrew to consider their verdict which, when it was delivered, read as follows:-

> That George Warren, on 24th May 1901, in the parish of Eglwysilan, in the County of Glamorgan, at the Universal Colliery, met with his death by burns and suffocation by the afterdamp resulting from an explosion at the said colliery on 24th May 1901, but we are unable to locate the exact spot, or to form an opinion as to how it originated, but agree that it was carried through the workings by coal dust

Their rider ran:-

> The jury considers that the colliery was not watered in a satisfactory manner, and would suggest that the present pipes be at once extended to the points recommended by Mr Gray.

> The jury does not consider that the system of watering by casks and allowing the water to run along the centre of the road is in any way sufficient and would in this case also suggest the use of an appliance similar to the one proposed by Mr Gray. The jury strongly urges the Members of the British Parliament to make it strictly compulsory to have the bottom, sides and top of the roads of collieries so well watered as to make it impossible for coal dust to spread an explosion.
> The jury also condemns the present system of giving out the explosives, and considers that a correct record should be kept of all explosives issued, used and returned.

(Gray's recommendation about watering the roads other than by casks was that this should be more effectively done by using an appliance similar to a street watering cart but which spread the water over a wider area and, to some extent, wet the sides as well as the floor of the roadways.)

The jury's deliberations ended with their 'expression of sympathy with the relatives of all who had lost their lives and with those of the young man, William Parker, whose body is still not found.'

The verdict, with its riders, accorded with the directions of the Coroner and reflected the opinions and evidence of the expert witnesses — if not of the colliery company representatives. Also its pronouncement paved the way for the reports required by the Home Secretary from the Inspector of Mines, J. T. Robson and from S. T. Evans, KC, MP.

Robson submitted his report on 15th November 1901 and Evans his on 12th December 1901.

Much of what was contained in the two reports has already been described in this narrative and in all the important details, apart from the site of origin of the explosion, confirmed the major aspects and recommendations in Galloway's report.

Robson's report examined, in particular, the probable cause and origin of the explosion but provided no conclusion. From his examination of the Pretoria District he was convinced that the explosion was not caused by shot firing there, nor could he find evidence that it was started anywhere by an open or defective miner's lamp.

He decided against Galloway's contention that it was caused by a shot fired by the Fullerloves, basing this on the evidence that their bodies were found over a hundred yards away along a straight road, when they could have gone into a near side road to await the firing of the shot. Additionally he noted the Doctor's evidence that they had lived probably five to ten minutes after the explosion. He was in full accord with the Inquest jury's verdict and strongly supported their recommendation for fresh legislation quoting a universal admission 'that coal dust is a "greater enemy" than even firedamp.'

The report by S. T. Evans was directed mainly at considering the five questions he posed:-

1. What control was exercised over the explosives used for shot firing?
2. How were the operations of shot firing regulated and exceeded?
3. What precautions were taken to allay and water the dust in the immediate vicinity of the shots before they were fired?
4. What was done to clear the dust in the chief roadways in the mine so as to prevent the accumulation of fine coal dust?
5. What steps were taken to water the roads, or render innocuous, so far as might be, the dust which must be made in such a colliery, so as to restrict or limit the extent of any explosion that might, unfortunately, take place?

Evans found laxity in the control over explosives, lack of supervision over shot firing and the attendant watering procedures, a lack of appreciation by the management of the need to clear coal dust from roads, and that roads had been inadequately watered. In his own report to the Home Secretary he went on to say:-

> If the explosion had occurred when the 240 night men were all in the mine, or in the day time when about 450 men would be below ground, it will be seen that upon the efficiency of the watering of the coal dust might have depended hundreds of lives.

He concluded:-

> While there was some laxity upon the matters to which reference has been made, I do not think there was established any breach of specific statutory duties to which the explosion was due, and I do not recommend any prosecution . . . It appears to me to be most desirable that stricter regulations should be made for the control and use of explosives in mines, and for limiting as far as possible, or practicable, shot firing during shifts; and especially that provisions should be made for preventing the accumulation of coal dust, and for the regular and efficient watering of the roads, roofs, and sides in the main haulage and travelling ways in mines which were dry and dusty.

The lessons literally being shouted at the coal mining industry in general, and the owners and management of the Universal Colliery in particular, by Professor Galloway, the inquest jury, the Mines Inspectors and S. T. Evans were both clear and simple. The message was that:-

- coal dust and air was a mixture of bombshell potential
- haulage roads would continue to be powder magazines for this explosive mixture as long as trams were over-filled, liable to spillage, and not dust-tight
- effective watering could neutralise and eliminate the explosive propensities of coal dust, and this should be made a legal requirement
- the Universal Colliery was a dry, dusty and gassy mine and would always be a source of danger unless adequate safety precautions were taken and rigorously maintained
- in such a mine any uncontrolled flame or spark, whether originating from a fired shot or by accident, could be a source of potential danger and detonate an explosion affecting all the workings.

Eighty-one men had died, horribly and disgustingly, to provide the basis for these elementary truths. Events in the mining industry between 1901 and 1913 were to provide reminders of these elementary lessons and would prove on 14th October 1913 how well the lessons had been learned — or ignored.

Chapter 7

Reminders, Warnings and Lessons ignored

LONG BEFORE the jury had produced their indecisive conclusions on the cause and source of the explosion, and their pointed recommendations about the control of explosives and coal dust, life for many in the valley had resumed the pattern familiar to them before that fateful May morning. But for the minority — the dependants and relatives of the eighty-one men who died — their shattered life pattern needed to be reformed with the notable omission of the centrepiece of the dead wage earner. For the rest of their lives they were to be affected by the misery associated with sudden death and the ever present threat of poverty attending the elimination of a breadwinner's earning capacity. His presence in the family could never be restored whilst his wages would be supplanted, in part only, by the cold charity of official funds and public benevolence.

From these the most dependants could expect were the meagre payments under the Workmen's Compensation Act and, from the South Wales Miners' Appeal Fund, ten shillings (50p) per week for an adult dependant and five shillings (25p) for a child.

The payment under the provisions of the Workmen's Compensation Act of 1897 were scaled according to the wages of the dead miner and the extent to which those now bereft had been dependent upon him — savouring of a sliding scale for bereavement.

For relatives wholly dependent on the wage earner the Act provided for the payment of 'a sum equal to his earnings in the employment . . . during the three years preceding the injury (causing death), or the sum of one hundred and fifty pounds, whichever of those sums is the larger, but not exceeding in any case three hundred pounds . . .' This put the value of a dead husband and father between £150 and £300.

For relatives partly dependant on the victim the payment was an amount to be agreed on, but not exceeding the £150 to £300 limits. Where disagreement was registered the question was determined by arbitration.

Victims with no dependants could rest in their graves assured of the payment of 'reasonable expenses for medical expenses and burial, not exceeding ten pounds.'

For William Harris, the lone survivor, payment during his incapacity was limited to half his usual wages up to a maximum of one pound per week.

The majority in the valley were not affected by these considerations except that, as workmates, neighbours and friends, their close proximity to those bereaved made them aware of the paucity of the payments. Workmates recognised their own fortunate evasion of the explosion and its consequences was due entirely to either an accident of time or of shift allocation in the colliery. For them the return to normality was aggravated by a sense of anger at the level of compensation enacted as adequate for loss of life in one of the most dangerous of occupations. Whilst they acknowledged and accepted disaster and sudden death as an occupational hazard of coal mining its presence had previously been manifested in other pits and other valleys. Now it had struck the Aber Valley — and the consequences were becoming apparent.

Any major mining disaster shatters the tenor of the community's life and immediately after it there is a period of frenzied but controlled activity when coal owners, management and workmen co-operate and bend all their efforts to find and rescue those trapped underground. Where rescue fails, or hope is abandoned, the effort is directed at the recovery of bodies for decent burial, for there is something inexplicably obscene to a mining community in the abandonment of the bodies of any of its members in colliery workings. It smacks of failure and a breach of loyalty so much so that, even today, when recounting details of long past disasters where this happened miners will add, in conscionable recrimination, a comment that so many bodies 'are still down there.'

The bond of united purpose between masters and workmen during the period of rescue and retrieval is transient and disappears quickly. It is replaced first by an angry call for retribution and then by the underlying sense of distrust normally existing between men and masters. In Senghenydd the cracks began to appear soon after 3rd June following the breaching of the falls blocking entry into the Pretoria District. The break into Pretoria confirmed the estimated death roll and left little else for the powerful flood of effort to batter against.

Any question of retribution for owners or management was ultimately thwarted by the inconclusive inquest findings with no apparent culpable breach of the legal requirements.

Thus, life in Senghenydd soon began to resume the pattern it knew before May 1901. The demand for Welsh coal was still increasing rapidly and its winning and export — especially from the easily worked seams in the Universal Colliery — were major influences in accelerating the return to the erstwhile familiar and normal. Evidence of this demand is apparent in the increased output of the South Wales coal field from over 29 million tons in 1901 to 56 million tons in 1913. The colliery at Senghenydd added its own quota to this increase with the annual production of nearly 184,000 tons in 1901 being increased to over 500,000 tons by 1913. By that year the work force on the day shift — the coal winning shift — had increased from 450 to 950, and the population of the two villages had trebled to about 11,000.

In the mine the existing districts on both east and west sides of the shafts had expanded and been extended. On the east side the Nine Feet seam had been opened up and was being worked from a landing about 560 yards down the shaft. To the west the original districts of Ladysmith, Kimberley, Mafeking and Pretoria had been enlarged as they had eaten their way outwards from the York and Lancaster shafts. Two new districts. — the Bottanic, north-west of the shafts, and the West York to their south-west — had been opened and were featuring in the mine's increased production. In opening the Bottanic District the road known as No 1 North had been extended to connect the Lancaster Level with the East Side Main Level. This road connected west side and east side whilst by-passing the York and Lancaster shafts.

Coal was undoubtedly King during this period and there is little wonder that, in the coal rush, the explosion of 1901 with its lessons was soon forgotten. Yet in these twelve years there were a number of separate events which time was to prove were particularly pertinent to conditions in the Senghenydd mine.

The first affected the use of electricity in mines. By the beginning of the century electricity was being used increasingly underground. Mainly it was used for lighting and, occasionally, to power small machines, with all the danger attending short circuiting, sparking, severed cables and electrocution.

In October 1902 the Home Secretary appointed Henry H. S. Cunynghame, an Assistant Under Secretary in the Home Office, to head a departmental committee. They were required to 'enquire into the use of electricity in coal mines and the danger attending it; and to report what courses should be adopted in the interest of safety by the establishment of Special Rules or otherwise.'

They reported that the use of electricity underground was felt to be as potentially dangerous as using explosives. Consequently they recommended that such electrical plant should be of good quality and ought to be enclosed 'to prevent gas being fired by sparking.' Also, it should be in the charge of competent persons. These requirements were incorporated into a set of Special Rules issued to coal mines by the Home Office in 1905.

However, the passage of time blunts the edge of all rules and fogs the danger they seek to nullify. But, in this case further reminders were to be forthcoming before 1913 about the danger of electrical power in gassy and dusty mines and, at the investigation into the cause of the 1913 explosion at Senghenydd, long and exhaustive enquiries were made into the possibility that the sparking of the underground electrical signalling system fused the explosion which brought so much sorrow to the Aber Valley.

Just over two years after the Committee's report was published a coal mining disaster in France shook the mining world with the enormity of its death roll. Also, it provided grim and fearful evidence of the fiery fulminating properties of coal dust.

On 10th March 1906 in the Pas de Calais coal field the Courrieres Mine erupted with an explosion that affected five of the thirteen shafts in use at the mine and killed 1,230 miners and 97 horses. The loss of life was on such a scale to incite the Home Secretary to seek a report on the disaster so that its implications could be studied to prevent anything similar happening in Britain. The preparation of this report again fell to Henry H. S. Cunynghame of the Home Office. He was assisted by W. N. Atkinson, an Inspector of Mines, and their report was presented to Parliament on 13th September 1906.

It stressed that the Courrieres mine was 'singularly free from firedamp, so much so that it was in great part worked with naked lights.' This gave added weight to the conclusion that 'the explosion was an extensive and very formidable dust explosion, without in all probability, the presence of any gas.'

As far as the source of the explosion was concerned the report favoured a conclusion that it could have been due to the accidental detonation of a shot that had previously misfired. At the time the report was written the French were investigating the possibility of an explosion of firedamp; Cunynghame and Atkinson commented on this. They pointed out that opinions might differ on the presence, or otherwise, of firedamp

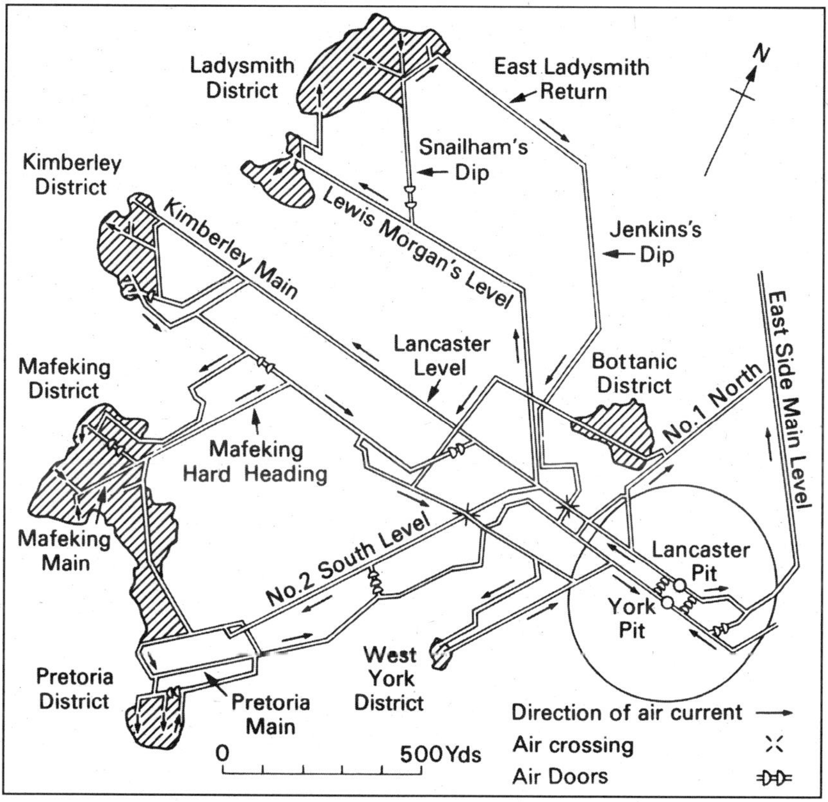

3. Universal Colliery, the West Side, 14th October 1913

when the explosion originated 'but the point that is of supreme importance is the consideration that, however originated, an explosion can travel over the whole extent of a mine by coal dust alone, and without any gas. And this we have no doubt whatever was the case at Courrieres.'

The report warned that the explosion emphasised the danger — recognised as existing in similar dry and dusty mines in Britain — could well result in a British disaster equalling that at Courrieres, unless action was taken to water or remove dry coal dust from the roads in mines. Prophetic words, indeed!

The implications of the French disaster were such that three months before the publication of the report, a Royal Commission was set up in June 1906 under Lord Robert Monkswell. Among its eight members were Henry Cunynghame, Sir Lindsay Wood, William Abraham (Mabon), and Robert Smillie, the President of the Lancashire Miners' Union.

Their commission was to advise the Home Secretary:-

> Whether it is desirable to make compulsory the watering of the roads in dry and dusty mines.
> Whether steps could be taken for the prevention of accidents, particularly those from the use and firing of explosives, from falls of roof and sides, from underground haulage and from winding.
> Whether any special provision should be made to facilitate the work of rescue in the event of an accident; and whether any improvement can be made in the present system of investigation and inquiry into accidents.

These superficially innocuous questions were to occupy the Commission for nearly five years, to involve their taking evidence from all interested parties in the mining industry, to produce three massive volumes of closely printed minutes of evidence and to result in three separate reports by them in 1907, 1909, and 1911. These reports formed the basis for the Coal Mines Act of 1911 — and it was against the legal requirements of this Act that the owners and management of the Universal Colliery were to be judged following the explosion in 1913.

The Commission's first report was published as Command Paper 3548 on 30th May 1907 and covered their detailed examination of all types of breathing apparatus in use in mines. Their main recommendation was that: 'Each working will provide on the spot a minimum of two appliances and eight persons having a thorough knowledge of the mine.' *Working* in this context could be interpreted as a group of mines with a central rescue station serving them and providing appliances and assistance to individual collieries. In 1913 the colliery at Senghenydd had three rescue teams but no breathing apparatus.

The next report by the Commission was published in July 1909 (as Comd 4820) and covered an impressive range of nearly twenty mining functions and subjects. The scope of the subjects they dealt with reflected the extent of the Royal Commission's application to their task and their wide interpretation of the questions before them.

Of particular importance and relevance to the happenings at Senghenydd in 1913 were their comments and recommendations relating to Inspection by Firemen and Deputies; Ventilation; Coal Dust Explosions; the Control of Coal Dust, including the Use of Dust-tight Tubs; and the Investigation of Accidents. All these matters were to figure largely in both the inquest and inquiry hearings that were to take place later in Senghenydd.

On inspection of working places by firemen and deputies the Commission recommended that 'the size of districts should be such as to enable the men appointed to carry out in a thorough manner all the duties imposed on them . . . the fireman or deputy should be enabled to give his whole time and attention to duties immediately concerned with the safety of the workmen under his charge.'

The size of the districts allocated to the firemen in the Universal Colliery came in for severe criticism at the ensuing investigation in 1913. It was contended they were too large to permit adequate checks for safety.

On the question of ventilation the Commission heard evidence how 139 men died in 1893 in the Combs Pit at the Thornhill Colliery near Dewsbury; how 35 men died at the Whitwick Colliery, Leicestershire in 1898 and how 28 men died at the Hamstead Colliery, Staffordshire in March 1908 because the current of air through these mines could not be reversed following fires and explosions. Consequently, they stressed 'the importance of collieries being provided with means of reversing the air current in the event of fire or explosion.

This was written into the 1911 Coal Mines Act, which was to require all collieries with mechanical ventilation to provide by the first day of January 1913 means for reversing the air current through the mine. At Senghenydd, due to the structural alterations needed, this date was extended to 30th September 1913. Fourteen days later, when the explosion occurred, this requirement had still not been met.

Although eighteen men were rescued from the mine without the air current being reversed, the unanswerable question which occupied every mind was how many more men would not have suffocated in the workings in the Universal Colliery if the air current had been immediately reversible.

In dealing with the explosive properties of coal dust the Commission found that Galloway's assertions were confirmed by all the witnesses they questioned. They reported:- 'The witnesses, who included those best qualified . . . to speak on the question . . . were generally agreed on two points — that coal dust is liable to explosion with or without the presence of firedamp and that there is a pressing case for the elucidation of the problems involved by a series of exhaustive experiments on an adequate scale.' They recorded with concern that there was an element among management that still refused to acknowledge the proven danger in coal dust.

However, when they examined and commented on the control of coal dust underground, they found they were dealing with a complex problem to which there was not a simple single solution.

The major source of dust, they found, was from defective tubs or trams. (Here again Galloway's contentions in his 1901 report were being confirmed). The Commission reported that loading coal above the level of the sides of the trams was still prevalent in South Wales and to prevent spillage of coal or dust they recommended care in loading, the use of dust-tight trams and water spraying of loaded trams in transit.

Evidence about the control of coal dust showed that methods used were various and diverse. Among the different methods advocated were: ensuring that roof, sides and roadways be made as smooth as possible to prevent any accumulation of dust; watering of roof, sides and floor; spreading hygroscopic deliquescent salt to lay the dust; and mixing shale or stone dust with the coal dust. Whilst all these were commendable under certain conditions, objections were registered against every one of them as a universal solution. For example, in some areas it was said that the watering of floor, roof and sides of roads resulted in a softening of the strata and its ultimate collapse. Nevertheless there was general agreement on the need to ensure that some acceptable method of control of coal dust be devised.

Time and time again, either directly or by implication, the conditions resulting in the explosion at Courrieres were quoted and experienced witnesses forecast a similar happening in England. For example (in answer to Question 6416), Mines Inspector W. N. Atkinson said that, in the absence of watering, an explosion with the same loss of life as at Courrieres was possible in England. Similarly, R. D. Bain, Mines Inspector for the Durham District, saw the possibility of all the day shift men in an English pit being killed in these circumstances.

These were prophetic utterances which were to see realisation all too soon in Wales rather than England.

In view of the diversity of methods recommended to them for the control of coal dust the Commission were obliged to report:-

> Experiments on a large scale are required before the Commission can come to any decision . . . and we recommend that they should be undertaken without delay.

They recorded that these experiments were already in hand with the Mining Association of Great Britain but until the results were available 'we are unable to make any final recommendations on the subject of watering or other means of dealing with coal dust.'

As it was, their exhaustive enquiries into the sources of coal dust, its spillage from trams, and its control and clearance underground resulted in Section 62 of the Coal Mines Act of 1911 requiring:-

> PREVENTION OF COAL DUST
> 62. In every mine, unless the floor, roof, and sides of the roads are naturally wet throughout, — . . .
> (2) the tubs shall be constructed and maintained as to prevent, as far as practicable, coal dust escaping through the sides, ends or floor of the tubs, but any tub which was in use in any mine at the date of the passing of this Act may, notwithstanding that it is not so constructed, continue to be used in that mine for a period of five years from the said date;
> (3) the floor, roof and sides of the roads shall be systematically cleared so as to prevent, as far as practicable, coal dust accumulating;
> (4) such systematic steps, either by way of watering or otherwise, as may be laid down by the regulations of the mine shall be taken to prevent explosions of coal dust occurring or being carried along the roads;
> (5) the roads shall be examined daily and a report (to be recorded in a book kept at the mine for that purpose) made on their condition as to coal dust and on the steps taken to mitigate danger arising therefrom.

These requirements — reflecting the lessons preached by Galloway — were to be the subject of intensive questioning and examination when the inquiry into the 1913 explosion took place. Also, they were destined to be the basis on which criminal charges were laid against the colliery company and the manager.

The only other recommendation of note contained in the Commission's second report affected the procedure for the investigation of accidents. What they recommended was: 'Wherever possible an accident should be investigated at the Coroner's inquest so as to avoid the necessity for further inquiry, but in some cases it would be advisable for a formal inquiry to be made . . . The matter should be left to the discretion of the Secretary of State.'

The happenings at Senghenydd on 14th October 1913 were to be the subject of both a Coroner's inquest and a judicial inquiry by the Secretary of State. Which of these should have precedence was to cause some dissension when it appeared they would run nearly concurrently. It was resolved when the Coroner insisted that, as the Crown's representative, his court was superior.

The Commission's third and final report was published as Command Paper 5561 in February 1911 and was mainly concerned with the treatment of pit horses and ponies.

The recommendations in the three reports found their way onto the statute books in the Coal Mines Act of 1911 which was enacted on 16th December 1911. The Act was a major step forward towards uniformity of practice in mines and in ensuring the safety of the thousands then working in the industry. Its scope and compass was a tribute to the exhaustive enquiries painstakingly carried out by the Commission and their intelligent interpretation of the dangers attending the mining of coal.

However, before the Royal Commission completed reporting on their findings two other events took place which were to be of significance for safety in mines in general and in the Universal Colliery in particular.

In October 1910 the colliery again demonstrated its gaseous, fiery nature and its potential for producing an unexpected and dangerous situation when a blower of gas occurred in the Mafeking Level. The blower was of such magnitude to require the immediate withdrawal of all the miners working in the mine and their exclusion from the workings for four days while the gas was cleared.

Two months later, in December, a Home Office Departmental Committee, appointed in 1909, reported on their inquiry into the working of the existing Special Rules for the use of Electricity in Mines, and recommended the amendments they felt were now necessary to those rules. (The Chairman of the Committee was R. A. S. Redmayne, Chief Inspector of Mines. He was destined to inquire into the 1913 explosion at Senghenydd and to comment on the mine's electrical signalling systems).

What the Committee had found was that the original application of electricity for lighting and small motors had been replaced by its use for nearly every operation requiring mechanical power in or about a colliery. They saw that this extension in the use of electricity underground also increased the risk of danger from electrical installations. The main dangers were those of explosion of coal dust and/or gas by open sparking, and of electric shock.

To counteract these dangers they recommended that electricity should be excluded from all those parts of mines where gas, in detectable quantities, was found daily or frequently. Where gas was rarely or never found electricity could be used providing open sparking capable of igniting gas etc. was obviated as far practicable. The only dangers in such 'gas free' areas was an unexpected blower of gas or a dense cloud of coal dust coinciding with sparks from the apparatus. (Of such coincidences were disasters born!)

On the danger of electric shock they agreed that even moderate voltages, in the conditions existing underground, could be dangerous to life and it was imperative that the apparatus used there should be so constructed, installed and maintained that, as far as was practicable, the danger of shock was removed.

These findings were reflected in changes which were made to the Special Rules and the most important of these in its relation to the Senghenydd Colliery, was Rule 15(i), which ran:-

> (15) The use of Electricity where Inflammable Gas may be present.
> In any part of a mine in which inflammable gas, although not normally present, may occur in quantity sufficient to be indicative of danger, the following additional rules shall be observed:
> (i) All cables, apparatus, signalling wires and signalling instruments shall be constructed, protected and worked, so that in the normal working thereof there shall be no risk of open sparking

Within two years the good sense of this requirement was to be brought home in tragic circumstances at a colliery not far from Senghenydd.

On 27th March 1912 at Bedwas Colliery about a mile or so from Caerphilly, an explosion injured twelve men, three of whom were destined to die of their burns. The ensuing investigation decided the explosion had been triggered off by the ignition of gas from the open sparking of the signalling system. The implications for safety in the gassy mines of South

Wales were of such importance to move W. N. Atkinson, Mines Inspector, to write to all mine owners in the following terms:-

> 123 Cathedral Road
> Cardiff
>
> 28th August 1913
>
> Gentlemen
> I am directed by the Secretary of State to inform you that an explosion of firedamp occurred recently in the South Wales Inspectors Division, by which 12 men were burnt, 3 of them so severely that they subsequently died.
> The explosion was proved beyond all reasonable doubt to have been caused by the sparking of an electrical signalling bell which ignited an accumulation of gas resulting from a derangement of the ventilation due to the breakage of air pipes.
> It was afterwards proved experimentally that sparks from the bell in question worked by a battery of 11½ volts would ignite an explosive mixture of lighting gas and air, and the mixture was also ignited by sparks from signalling wires produced by a current of only 4 volts pressure.
> I am instructed therefore to call your attention to the necessity of strict observance of Electrical Special Rule 15(i) with reference to signalling apparatus.
>
> Yours faithfully,
> W. N. ATKINSON

It has already been pointed out that the signalling system in use in the Universal Colliery in 1913 was one that produced open sparking.

It can be argued with some justification that hind-sight probably endues this catalogue of happenings, reports and requirements with a degree of relevance and importance they did not attract as they occurred in the period between 1901 and 1913. Nevertheless they each had a bearing on what happened in Senghenydd in October 1913 and need to be instanced to allow a reader to form his own opinion whether any failure to recognise their significance implies blame on coal owners, management, trade unions or workmen. This required knowledge also of the events in Senghenydd on Tuesday, 14th October 1913.

Chapter 8

THE SORROW OF SENGHENYDD
A day of numbing shock
Tuesday, 14th October 1913

AT FOUR O'CLOCK in the morning of Tuesday, 14th October 1913 fourteen year old Harry Wedlock was wide awake after a night's sleep both fitful and disturbed. He was due to start work in an hour or so as a colliery boy at the Senghenydd mine working with Sydney Gregory of 24 Station Terrace, Senghenydd, and the mixture of apprehension and excitement he felt about his first job had affected his sleep.

The excitement of a boy new from school going to his first job was natural; his apprehension was born of the unknown entailed in working far below ground in the darkness of strange surroundings where danger was always near. Friends had warned him of the stomach-wrenching drop of the cage in its descent into darkness. He had been primed on the jokes and leg-pulls perpetrated by miners on a new boy and felt he knew how to deal with requests to fetch a bucket of 'blast' (compressed air) or to get some 'glass wedges' to ease the coal from its seam.

By 4:45am his mother had given him breakfast and seen him out of the house in his unfamiliar working clothes and complete with his tin 'tommy box' of bread and cheese and his 'jack' of cold tea.

As he made his way up the valley through the darkened streets of Abertridwr and Senghenydd towards the mine at the head of the valley, he was joined by other boys and men. They were all making their way to the colliery prior to descending the pit when winding began at 5:10am. It was a day little Harry Wedlock would remember all his life.

From 51 Caerphilly Road in Senghenydd William Joseph Hyatt and his three sons set out together on their short walk to the pit. William and his son, Brynley, worked in the west side of the colliery whilst the other two

The Universal Colliery on the morning of 14th October 1913
(permission of the National Museum of Wales)

sons, Charles and William, worked on the east. It was destined to be their last walk together.

From 18 Alexandra Terrace a father and 14 year old son, both named Charles Baker, made their way down the hill to the colliery below them to join the men waiting around the colliery yard. They were not to return at the end of the day, and the elder Baker was not to see again the baby his wife had given birth to on the previous Saturday.

From all over the little valley men and boys converged on the colliery, obtained their lamps from lamp room attendant William Morse and then congregated in groups around the head of the Lancaster pit. There they waited for John Mogridge, the banksman, to usher them in to cages and signal the winder for their descent.

Within an hour all 950 of those working below ground had been lowered down the pit and most of them were preparing for or had started work. About 440 of these day shift workers were men in the districts on the west side of the mine. With the workforce safely below ground the banksman and the winders turned their attention to winding up coal and lowering empty trams and supplies to the workers underground.

By eight o'clock everything was working normally and smoothly as evident in the normal gyration of the wheels on the winding gear. Edward Shaw, the manager, satisfied that this was to be another uneventful day, strolled over to the lamp room to talk to lamp room man Morse. At ten minutes past eight, as they were talking, they heard a terrific explosion accompanied by the scream and clash of rending metal, the splintering of baulks of timber followed by the thud and clang of falling debris. Shaw rushed out to see a cloud of dust and smoke rising around the headgear of the Lancaster pit

Once again the pit had erupted blasting a cage up the shaft, rocketing it into the headgear and wrecking the timber platform at the surface. The wrecked platform had exploded beneath the feet of John Mogridge, the banksman, and the rising splintering timber had severed his head from his body fountaining blood in crimson patches on the crow black grime around the 'bank.' As Teddy Shaw arrived at the mouth of the Lancaster pit surface workers were already moving Mogridge's body whilst the clouds of fumes and dust from the pit mouth were beginning to clear. He saw that the cage was seriously damaged with the ironwork of the bottom and sides wrenched and buckled; the corrugated roof around the pit had been blasted away and now lay drunkenly awry. In those first moments he must have realised this was the nightmare of 1901 all over again — with all the indications that it would be even worse. All his day shift officials were below ground and there was no-one immediately at hand to share responsibility for the multiplicity of things calling for attention. This was the loneliness of the man at the top with a vengeance.

But accounts of his ensuing actions indicate that he kept his head and did all that one man could in those lonely and panic-fraught circumstances — although, inevitably, some criticism was later levelled at the time which elapsed before he summoned rescue brigades with breathing apparatus and before they appeared on the scene.

From the Lancaster pit Shaw crossed to the York pit and checked that all was in order at the surface there. What he saw assured him he had at least one workable shaft to provide an avenue of escape for those underground. Next he checked with Benjamin Price, the fan engineman, that the fan was working properly and the ventilation was being maintained. In normal circumstances the fan turned at constant speed but any obstruction — from explosion, fire or falls — would cause a check in the speed and indicate that something was wrong. With the assurance that ventilation appeared to be in order Shaw gave instructions to the pit mechanic to repair the damage to the top of the Lancaster shaft and to take out the buckled cage and replace it with another.

By this time men, women and children from the two villages, alerted by the explosion, were converging on the mine in their hundreds to seek news and offer help. One of the first officials to appear was David R. Thomas, a night overman, and he immediately volunteered to accompany Shaw in a descent of the York pit to assess the conditions underground. Shaw gave instructions to lower the cage slowly so they could check the air they encountered was fit to breathe. This was a necessary precaution because smoke was rising out of the pit. When they had descended about 15 yards the banksman received a signal from the pit bottom and hauled them back to the surface. To Shaw the news of signals from the east side was good news indeed — it was news of survivors below.

Shaw and Thomas, now joined by other men, began the slow descent again and, as they met the ascending cage, saw in it the body of a man in a tram with his legs hanging over the crossbars. They signalled to stop the cages, crossed over into the other and pulled in the body; then they continued their descent to the Six Feet landing, 530 yards down. Here they found descent was halted by girders jamming the shaft, but by shouting down the shaft to the Nine Feet seam level about 20 yards below them on the east side, they were assured by the replies that some of the men on that side were safe.

Shaw's plan was to try to get into the main road, the Lancaster Level running from the Lancaster shaft, where all the signs indicated the main effects of the explosion would be seen. (See plan on page 78.) His plan was to go west from the York pit along the return road and cross to the Lancaster Level through the west cross-cut, some 40 yards from pit bottom. This was thwarted by the volume of smoke coming out of the return road so he decided to try the longer way round by going east from the York shaft and then through the other cross-cut about 45 yards east of the shaft. He found the east cross-cut on fire and the party were unable to enter it so they retraced their steps through the smoke-thick atmosphere to the York shaft, crossed over it and tried once more to enter the west cross-cut. Although this was also ablaze the fire was not as fierce as on the east side. They doused the fire as best they could, with eyes smarting and nearly choking with the all-pervading smoke, but finally got into the Lancaster Level and around to the Lancaster shaft.

About four yards away from the shaft they found Ernest Moses, a shackler, alive behind some empty trams. These must have shielded him from the blast which had rocketed the cage up the shaft and caused the death of eight men working around the shaft at pit bottom.

In the meantime the fire in the west cross-cut had again broken out and Shaw deputed David Thomas with a party of men to deal with it. Shaw himself, with another man, Jim George, made their way west along the Lancaster Level to see what conditions were like there.

Shaw's description of what he did and saw runs:-

> Well, when I got out on the Lancaster Level, we walked out west for, I should say, about 40 yards, till we came to the engine which was overhead, and there was a lot of planking and baulks about that engine, and these were beginning to blaze at the time. We succeeded in putting that fire out, and we went out further west again until we came to the crab engine, and there was a very heavy fire raging there. Beyond that point the arches ceased and it was all double timbering, and every pair of timbers as far as I could see was on fire . . . The timbers were on fire as far as I could see up to the entrance of No 1 North, and I saw we could do nothing there . . .

No falls of any magnitude had so far taken place 'but the laggings were just beginning to break down.' But Shaw knew that the collapse of the burning timbers would lead inevitably to massive falls in the main air intake road to the west side.

After David Thomas, the overman, saw it he described it as 'exactly like looking into a furnace.'

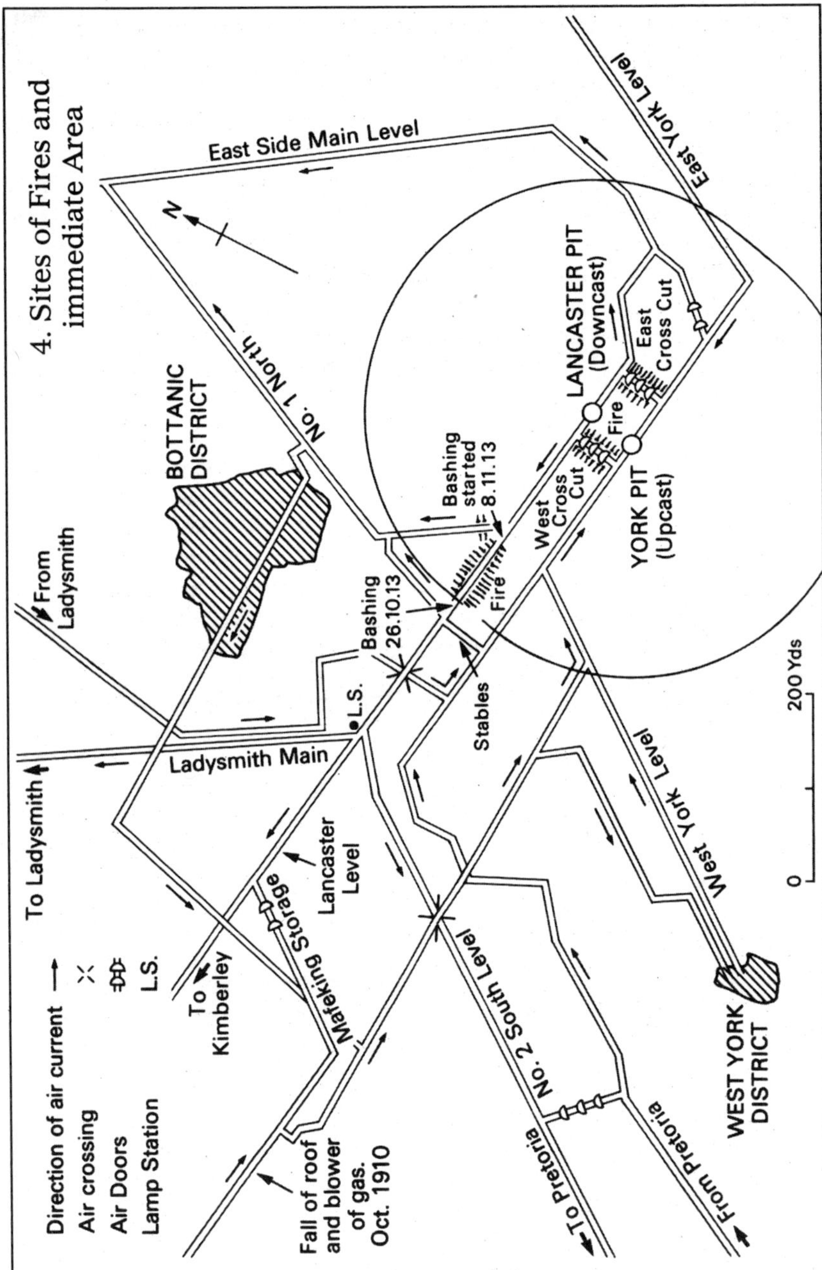

4. Sites of Fires and immediate Area

At that moment Teddy Shaw must have realised he had a major catastrophe on his hands and that there was little hope for the lives of the men working in the districts on the west side. He was looking at a raging fire on a main road which should have been taking clean air into the working places to the west of the Lancaster pit. Instead, suffocating smoke and noxious fumes generated by the fire were being swept into those working places — as confirmed by the smoke he had already met in the return road to the York pit when he twice tried to get through the west cross-cut. He could not rectify this by reversing the air current through the mine; the necessary structural alterations had not been made and reversal would take at least two hours — by which time the men on the west side could all have been suffocated. Furthermore, in reversing the air current, there was the danger of bringing out from the working places foul air and gas onto an established blaze, with the risk of another devastating explosion.

His despair, as he looked along the main road to the fire, must have been total.

There was little he could do on the west side and he returned to the east side where David Thomas and his party were fighting the fire in the east cross-cut. There he learned that all the men on the east side were safe and Thomas had instructed them to be withdrawn from the workings and brought to pit bottom. Shaw decided that instead they be kept back for about 100 yards from the shaft until he had cleared all the debris and trams blown into the shaft by the explosion. A party of men were detailed to do this whilst others gathered together all the injured men so that they could be sent to the surface first. When the east side men were eventually raised to safety about two hours later they were taken up in batches of twenty to twenty-eight.

Among the injured sent to the surface was William Henry Lasbury, as assistant timberman, who was found more dead than alive between the York shaft and west cross-cut. It took nearly four hours of artificial respiration in the carpenter's shop at the surface to revive him. He was rushed home and confined to bed for days — during this time no-one in authority at the colliery was told he had been brought out alive and, more importantly, that he had come out of the West York District. If this information had been known to the mining engineers and mines inspectors on the day of the explosion it could well have influenced a decision about reversing the air current through the colliery.

Lasbury's story, when it was told at the inquiry, was that he had descended the York pit that morning at about 7:50am and had made his way towards the West York District through the West York Return. About 20 yards or so below the engine in this road he was blown forward by blast and a cloud of dust. This put out his light and in the darkness he called to the engineman to ask if he was all right. The engineman shouted back to confirm he was, so Lasbury groped his way back towards the York shaft. When he drew near the west cross-cut he heard the sound of air rushing through the doors. Then, as he got nearer the cross-cut, the doors crashed open and disintegrated and splintered. He was knocked backwards by the blast but was not blown to the floor. When he recovered he again staggered back past the cross-cut towards the York shaft. By this time he had difficulty in breathing and eventually collapsed between the cross-cut and pit bottom. At the time he collapsed — about ten or fifteen minutes past eight — he saw no fire in the cross-cut. Lasbury remembered nothing more until he came to in the carpenter's shop some hours later.

His story intimated there had been two explosions — one when he was going towards the West York District and another when he was near the west cross-cut — but only one of these reached the surface to cause damage there. The similarity with the happenings in 1901 — when there was more than one explosion — was again being high-lighted. Other news Shaw received was that men and officials from the east side had tried to enter the No 1 North Level from the East Side Main Level — the No 1 North connected the main road into the east side districts with the Lancaster Level to the west — but they had been driven back because 'the smoke there was very, very thick.'

To Shaw this meant that all the ways into the west side were blocked by fire, fumes and smoke and, without breathing apparatus the only way in was through the furnace of the fire he had seen burning in the Lancaster Level. To overcome and douse that needed water and more water. And that was just not available.

Both shafts were fitted with a column of water pipes of 2 inch diameter — but the column in the Lancaster pit did not go right up to the surface. Some little way down the Lancaster shaft water seeped in — about 60 gallons per hour — and the pipe carried this down the shaft. In any case this column had been wrecked by the explosion and needed to be completely relaid if it was to bring water down to the fire. The pipe in the York shaft had been broken about 20 yards from the bottom but water was still flowing and had been used to extinguish the fire in the cross-cut on the east side. Shaw ordered the repair of this pipe and the laying from it of two lines of 1½ inch pipes into the Lancaster Level to fight the fire there.

(Under normal conditions the water column in each shaft adequately

The wrecked cage — after it had been blown up the Lancaster Shaft
('Daily Mirror photo, courtesy of Syndication International Ltd)

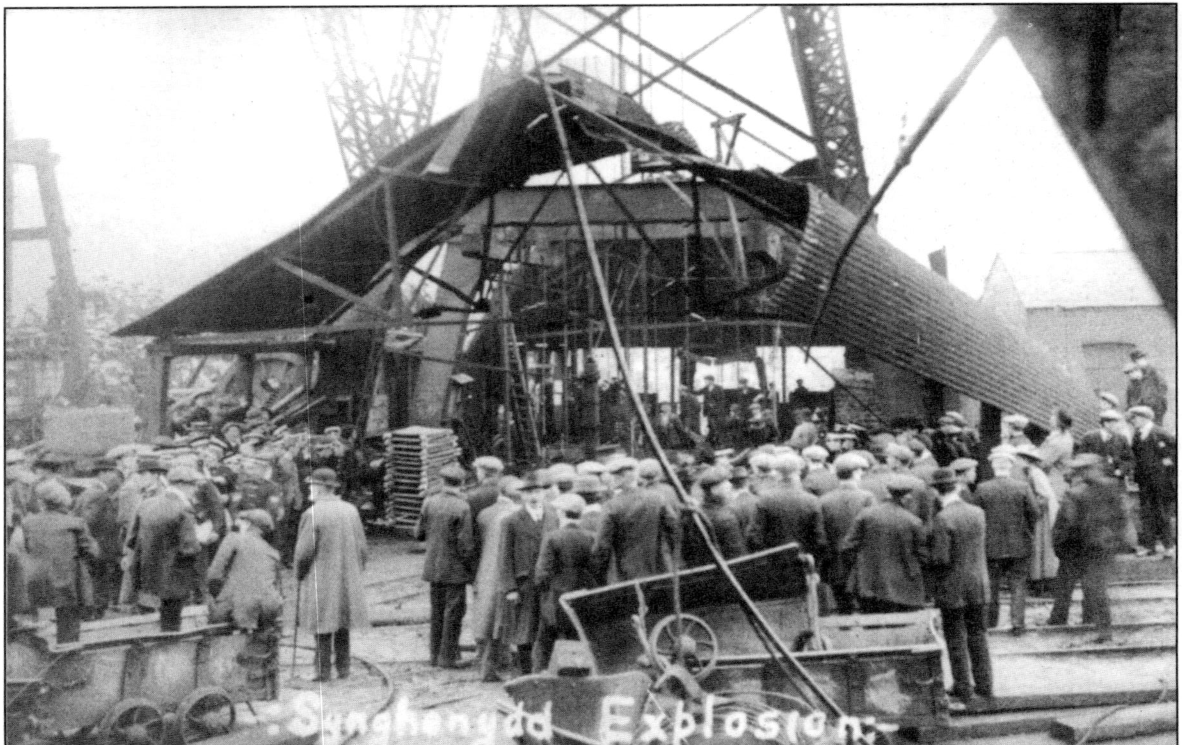

The wreckage around the pit-head of the Lancaster shaft caused by the explosion
(courtesy of Mrs A. Holder)

met the colliery's water needs below ground but, at the inquiry which followed, Shaw admitted it would have been advisable to have arranged to convey more water into the mine to meet the case of a possible fire. A case of being wise too late.)

It was now about 9:30am and he decided to go to the surface to call the rescue brigade with breathing apparatus from Porth, some 16 miles away by road; to inform Dr W. N. Atkinson, Inspector of Mines for the South Wales Division, and to arrange to augment the supply of water into the pit by laying pipes from a nearby reservoir.

By this time scores of men in the workings on the west side of the mine had already died in the blast of the explosion or been burned by the coal dust perpetuated flame which swept into their district. Others, missed by the blast and flames, were dying in the asphyxiating atmosphere generated by these twin killers.

In the Mafeking District, 14 year old Charles Baker, who had walked to work with his father of the same name, had died with him and now would be accompanying him only to their shared grave in Penyrheol cemetery.

On the east side many of the men working there realised something was radically amiss in the mine long before they were summoned to assemble at pit bottom to make their ascent to safety. One of the first men to come out of the stricken mine — even before Shaw ascended to call the rescue brigades — was Bert Walters of 2 Gelli Terrace, Senghenydd. 84 years old in 1979 he clearly remembers what happened that Tuesday morning.

He was working a few hundred yards east of the Lancaster pit just beyond a corner in the main level. Elias Morgan, the main roadman, was coming towards him from the Lancaster shaft and they were joined by Bill Jones coming from the east side. They heard a loud explosion and, not knowing what had happened, ran instinctively towards the Lancaster pit. They ran into a wall of dust and smoke which rendered Jones and Morgan unconscious. Their lights went out and Bert Walters was for a moment uncertain what to do for his colleagues. He decided to try to bring them around with a drink and groped his way back to get his water jack. Returning with it he revived his two mates and they decided to push on to the Lancaster shaft. Walters helped the other two over a fall partly blocking their way and ultimately they arrived at the shaft; here they found only one' man alive among the bodies around pit bottom. They decided to make their way to the York pit when they were met by Edward Shaw who asked Morgan what had happened. Morgan had to admit he did not know but added that whatever it was appeared to be serious. Seeing 18 year old

Walters, Shaw advised him to get up the shaft as quickly as possible.

His account continues:-

> So I went to the York pit. There wasn't a soul about and in the cage was a tram of rubbish and a tram with a body in it. I didn't know who it was but I decided to leave him there. Everything was so quiet I felt a bit afraid but I climbed on top of the rubbish and knocked to go up — my father was the banksman. As I was going up I wished I would get up before another explosion came. When I got to pit top there was hundreds of people there but I was taken home and examined by the doctor. He told me to go to bed in case there were any after-effects from gas, but I didn't stay there long. I went back to the pit in the afternoon to get news of my brother-in-law. It turned out he had been killed; my sister was the youngest woman to be widowed. She was twenty.

The fear felt, and admitted, by young Walters was shared by many that morning but, perhaps, more than most by little Harry Wedlock, the 14 year old in his first day in a doomed mine. Sidney Gregory recounted what happened and how he came to allay the fear felt by the boy.

> About 8am we heard two heavy thuds followed by a great deal of smoke. The air suddenly became still and this was followed by a lot of coal dust as thick as fog.
>
> A little boy from Aber, who started work as a colliery boy this morning, was with me and he started to cry and asked me what was the matter. I told him it would be all right. Later the fireman came and told us to go out. As we were going I could hear the fire raging. It was awful; the timber was cracking and falling and we could hardly stand the heat and foul air. The little boy was crying so I gave him some water and he got all right. At last we got to the bottom of the pit. There were a lot of colliers there but no-one seemed to know what happened. We were there nearly two hours and shortly after 10 o'clock we came to the surface.

This statement requires little imagination to envisage the appalling fear engendered in a young lad — or the tender protection and assurance he received from an adult miner facing the same unknown danger.

On the east side of the Lancaster pit the two brothers William and Charles Hyatt were working together in a heading when, shortly after 8am,

William noticed the air was gradually becoming foul and smoke laden. William consulted Charlie and they both agreed there was something radically wrong and they ought to check what was happening. They made their way to the East Side Main Level intending to get to the Lancaster pit but they were driven back by smoke. They then decided to get to pit bottom by going back along the East Side Main and then down to the Lancaster Level through the No 1 North. When they got to the No 1 North and went some way along it they could see a fire engulfing the road in the distance. William realised the fire was near where his father should be working with two or three boys — at that moment he also realised that there was little hope for his father and the others and voiced his fears to Charles. (Days later the bodies of William Hyatt Senior, with two other men and three boys were found near the No 1 North fire.)

Confronted by the impassable fire ahead of them the Hyatt brothers decided to go back to the East Side Main and try once more to get round to the Lancaster shaft. When they eventually returned to the east side they groped their way in the darkness — their lamps had been extinguished — and after nearly an hour they finally got to the York shaft. There they found two other men; with these they were raised to the surface.

Their other brother, Brynley, died in the Mafeking District and his body was not retrieved and identified until Wednesday, 17th November. William was so upset by this he was unable to go to his brother's funeral.

These three accounts are typical of others recounted by the men who came out of the mine safely that morning. All are stories of the initial realisation of the untoward and the ensuing cautious groping progress through fire, smoke and foul air to the safety of a cage to the surface and the bright sunlight of an October morning.

This gradual exodus from the workings towards the shaft was already in progress as Shaw was preparing to go up the pit at 9:30am. Before he left he gave instructions that when the work of clearance at pit bottom and in the shaft was finished a party was again to try to go round to the No 1 North through the East Side Main Level. Later in the day this party reported they had tried this again with breathing apparatus about 1pm but had been driven back by thick smoke. Thus, all ways into the west side still appeared to be blocked completely by smoke and fire.

After Shaw had summoned the rescue brigades and advised everyone concerned, including the Inspectors of Mines, he returned underground and continued to direct the clearance of the debris jamming the York shaft, the fighting with extinguishers of the fire in the Lancaster Level, and the repair of the water pipes. Work was hampered by the heat, the thick smoke and lack of breathing apparatus so that men had to be replaced at frequent intervals. Whilst volunteers were plentiful to provide these replacements, Shaw himself stayed underground to supervise the work in the choking smoke. Others came and went but Shaw remained. By 5pm he was virtually blind from the smoke and next morning a doctor took two hours to open his inflamed eyes. Soon after 10:30am Shaw's messages to rescue brigades, mines inspectors and others began to bring results. First to arrive were the Rhymney Valley rescue brigade, followed by those from Porth, Aberdare and Crumlin. About 11am the first Inspector of Mines, J. M. Carey, arrived, quickly followed by mining experts from all over the South Wales coal field. These included Thomas Griffiths, Leonard Llewellyn, David Hannah, D. Watts Morgan and James Winstone.

The rescue men were put to work to repair the broken water pipes in the west cross-cut where smoke had prevented all efforts to do this. The repair was possible only by the rescue men in their breathing apparatus concentrating all their electric lamps through the dense smoke on each repair point as they progressed through the cross-cut.

Men from the east side were now being sent up the York pit to safety and once they were cleared Shaw was able to direct attention to the repair of the fracture in the water column some 20 yards up the York shaft. This would provide more water to fight the fire in the Lancaster Level. Until the fire was conquered there was no hope of rescuers getting through to the west side to anyone still alive there.

By mid-day help was pouring into the little valley from all kinds of sources. A special detachment of police to control the crowds converging on the valley was brought in by special train laid on by the railway company; corps of St John and Red Cross workers came to help; Salvation Army soldiers and lasses, ever present in need and disaster, flocked to provide comfort; and Lord Merthyr and R. A. S. Redmayne, Chief Inspector of Mines, and Dr W. N. Atkinson, Mines Inspector for the South Wales Division, were on their way from London.

At 2pm Edward Shaw issued the first official statement — one that gave little indication of the severity of the disaster — which read:-

> At 8 o'clock this morning an explosion occurred at the Lancaster Pit of Messrs Lewis Merthyr Consolidated Collieries. There were 900 down the pit at the time. The workmen on the east side of the pit in Six Feet and Nine Feet seams have been brought up alive to the number of 489. There is a fire burning at the bottom of the downcast pit on

> the west side of it and it has been impossible so far to proceed beyond the fire. No workmen have been brought from the west side of the workings. Efforts are now being made to put out the fire.

The efforts being made were heroic in character. A blaze of terrifying proportion was being fought by men with hand extinguishers and insufficient water in a searing temperature they could stand only for two or three minutes at a time. Little wonder progress was painfully slow.

In the colliery yard men were engaged in making litters and stretchers ready to retrieve the injured and the dead whilst local undertakers had drawn on their stocks of coffins and piled them high to await the charred and blistered cadavers they were ultimately to encase. Eleven bodies had already been brought up and eight had been identified. Three of the injured had been taken to hospital; they were to die in hours. Senghenydd was still in the throes of hoping for the best while preparing for the worst.

Immediately Lord Merthyr arrived at the mine he called a meeting of all interested parties including Edward Shaw and all other mining engineers, the mines inspectors and representatives of the miners. This was with the intention of being apprised of the conditions underground and the action being taken to overcome them.

When Chief Inspector of Mines, R. A. S. Redmayne, arrived about 5:30pm he decided to go below, with Dr Atkinson, to see the situation for themselves. They found heavy falls had taken place on the Lancaster Level and the fire was burning beneath them — this fire was still being fought with water and fire extinguishers. Redmayne and Atkinson recommended the hot debris from the fire and falls be removed to the surface in trams and that a better supply of water be laid on to fight the fire. The removal of the red hot debris was started immediately and went on all through the night.

But once again, as in 1901, the assembled relatives and on-lookers were to have their hopes raised before they were finally destroyed.

At that time the impression among the mining engineers was that it was impossible to penetrate into the Bottanic District because of afterdamp and smoke. Redmayne was aware of this theory and he was concerned that gas from the Bottanic would seep back from the east side on to the fire. Consequently, he and Dr Atkinson gave instructions that ventilation on the east side of the pit be examined. This examination was made about 9pm that night by the two Mines Inspectors, T. Greenland Davies and P. T. Jenkins, with two mining engineers (not named). They discovered that air was going into the Bottanic District from the East Side Main Level instead of from the No 1 North. On their way back to the York pit Davies and Jenkins met Professor Redmayne and Clement Edwards MP, who were coming from the west side after inspecting progress with the fire fighting.

Davies told Redmayne what they had found and the party went back along the East Side Main Level towards the No 1 North and the Bottanic District as far as it was safely possible. In the road they found fresh horse droppings which had not been covered by dust. This led them to suppose that if a horse was alive in that area there was a strong probability that men would also be alive — if they could reach them in time. It was now about 9:30pm.

By 10pm arrangements had been made for a rescue party with breathing apparatus to go into the Bottanic District to seek and bring out any survivors. This party comprised R. T. Rees (agent to Lord Merthyr), Mines Inspector Greenland Davies, D. Watts Morgan (Miners Agent for the Rhondda Valley), Lewis Watkins (Manager of Bargoed Colliery) J. A. Price (Manager of Elliott's Colliery) D. W. Price (Mechanic, Rhymney) and Dr Daniel Thomas of Bargoed. The rescue men from the Rhymney Valley Rescue Station, under Superintendent Kitto, were Charles Williams, Thomas Griffiths, Benjamin Rees, F. C. Gregory, Thomas Reynolds and William Williams. The party was guided into the workings by Ted Harris, overman, and William Thomas, fireman.

The exploration was made by an advance party who maintained communications with the remainder acting as a standby in case of emergency. This advance party was made up of R. T. Rees, D. Watts Morgan, T. Greenland Davies, D. W. Price, Superintendent Kitto and Ted Harris. By 11:30pm they had made an entry into the workings in the Bottanic District and found a man and a young boy alive and uninjured.

A day of reviving hope — Wednesday, 15th October

This news reached the crowds thronging the pit-head at 1am that morning and later they were to have their spirits raised with the news that in all eighteen had been rescued.

D. Watts Morgan, Rhondda miners' agent recounted how they found young Evan Moore of Bedwas Road, Caerphilly and William Jones of 65 Hight Street, Senghenydd as they made their way into the Bottanic District — and their subsequent rescue of sixteen others.

> We found the little boy Moore and Jones in the Bottanic District on the west side about 1,200 yards from pit bottom. We were naturally delighted and gave a sort of cheer when we

Part of the large crowd waiting at the colliery for news
(courtesy of Mrs A. Holder)

> came across them. The little boy was groaning and was very weak — he was all but gone but we gave him artificial respiration and eventually got him round. We went through the district and altogether came across 18 men who were in a sort of shelter where they did not receive the full force of the blast. We attended to them and other rescuers gave them stimulants.

Of all the families favoured by fate by this rescue, the joy and relief felt by three of them had their own particular brand of sweetness.

Mrs Hill, of 15 Brynhyfryd, Senghenydd and a widow was overjoyed to find that her bread-winning 16 year old son, young James Hill, had been brought out alive. She alone could appreciate her good fortune in comparison with the plight of her neighbour next door at No 14. There the wife of James Thomas had been widowed and left with seven children, the eldest of whom was 16.

At 183 Caerphilly Road, Senghenydd, the rescue returned two brothers, John Owen Jones and Evan Jones, to the family fold. They were fortunate because in that road thirty-eight other men died in the explosion.

After finding young Evan Moore the rescue party went on to find his brother, George Moore, and their father – also called George Moore. The return of three men to a family was unique and when he recovered young George Moore was able to recount how he had been assisted and comforted by an older workmate. He told how Albert Dean, a married man with two children, had offered and made him take his last drop of tea. Dean was among the twenty who died in the Bottanic District.

Recently at his home in Claude Road, Caerphilly, 84 year old Evan Moore recalled what happened to him that day. Just before 8am his lamp went out and he spoke to his mate, William Jones — nicknamed 'Trawsfynydd' after his home village in North Wales — about going to the lamp station for a relight. At that moment there was a terrific bang and the ground shuddered under and around them. 17 year old Evan shouted, "there's something wrong, Traws! I'm not going for a light — let's get out!" They dashed back to their working place for their coats and joined the rush of men trying to get to pit bottom. They smelled smoke and eventually they had to turn back because the smoke was so thick and they could see fire ahead. As they went back towards the workings Evan Moore saw men stagger and, one by one, fall unconscious. He became dizzy himself and his last clear thought was 'I'm a goner.' He remembers falling and striking his forehead as he went down and landing with his face partly in a pool of horse's urine. He maintains that the proximity of his nose and mouth to this water was his salvation. He vaguely remembers hearing voices when he was found and recalls being taken to the St John Ambulance Hall at Aberdare Hall in Stanley Street, Senghenydd which had been set up as a temporary hospital. There he recovered with his younger brother, George, and his father.

The last man brought out alive among the eighteen rescued during the heroic search of the Bottanic District was Arthur Balsom of 17 Corbett Crescent, Caerphilly. After he had been resuscitated and brought to the surface he was able to recount what happened to him. He told how just after 8am he heard a terrific explosion and this was followed by a cloud of dust and smoke and his lamp went out. With others he rushed towards the Lancaster shaft but they were forced to retrace their steps when they were confronted with a fire. Eventually he found he was alone in the darkness and, to breathe more easily, he moistened his handkerchief with tea and covered his nose and mouth with it. Another man came up to him — Balsom did not say who this was — and Balsom gave him a drink. The man then left to try to find a way out and Balsom heard no more of him. Soon he felt dizzy and he lay down with his handkerchief over his face. He became unconscious and was found in that state by the rescue party.

The rescue party's success in finding and bringing out alive eighteen men was somewhat overshadowed by their recovery also of twenty bodies. But this in no way affected the acclaim of the thousands assembled around the pit-head when, with the eighteen safe at the surface, the rescue party finally stepped out of the cage in the early hours of Wednesday morning. According to any eye witness there were no cheers or applause from the waiting crowds; instead in complete silence they watched the rescue party's tired progress across the colliery with every man doffing his hat in knowledgeable recognition and homage of the rescuers' accomplishment. Many fell to their knees to offer a prayer of thanksgiving. The thunder of the crowd's silence reverberated through the hills of the little valley far louder than applause or cheers could ever do — it was an accolade born of knowledge and harsh experience of danger.

The recovery of twenty bodies concurrent with the rescue of the eighteen from the same district was destined to evoke doubt whether earlier exploration would have saved more lives. This doubt was expressed by Tom Richards MP, Secretary of the Miners' Federation. His utterance called for reply and during Wednesday it was forthcoming.

In a statement issued early in the day Lord Merthyr recorded the rescue in the Bottanic District and refuted any suggestion of delay in inspecting those particular workings; he pointed out that all the operations had been carried out in co-operation with and under the advice of the Inspectors of Mines and no time had been lost in implementing this advice. The report also recorded the intention to lay a new column of 2-inch water pipes down the Lancaster shaft. This only underlined the inadequacy of the existing water supply and the ferocity of the blaze below.

Efforts were still concentrated on controlling and subduing the fire in the Lancaster Level. These efforts claimed another life that Wednesday when William John of Thomas Street, Abertridwr, was buried beneath a heavy fall and killed instantly.

During the day it was decided to appoint a committee of mining experts (viz. Thomas Griffiths, David Hannah, Leonard Llewellyn, Tudor Davies and D. Watts Morgan with Edward Shaw and the Mines Inspectors) to oversee the fire-fighting, rescue and repair operations. They held a meeting at the colliery and decided to reduce the speed of the fan to cut down the air current to the fire whilst maintaining reasonable ventilation. After the meeting they issued a statement recording their resolution to do a number of things. These were:- to fight the fire with all the force of water possible; to bring out in trams all moveable burning material and, after the fire had been extinguished, to send in rescue men to examine the ventilation, air bridges and doors. The statement ended ominously with their opinion that no useful purpose would be served in sending rescue men into the workings. That was interpreted by many as the disappearance of hope.

However, the rescue from the Bottanic District offered one ray of hope. The district had been reached by men going along the East Side Main Level and then westerly through the No 1 North — this might provide a means of getting into the Lancaster Level behind or west of the fire raging there. But first the fire in the No 1 North itself had to be overcome.

This was to become the plan of action. But its success depended on the efficient ventilation of the Bottanic District and the No 1 North Level. This was speedily arranged by the construction and erection of ventilation doors to direct fresh air into the area, and followed by an attack with hand extinguishers on the fire in the No 1 North at its juncture with the Lancaster Level.

In London public attention was directed towards a much happier event in the marriage of Prince Arthur of Connaught to the Duchess of Fife. In consequence King George V was unable to realise his desire to visit Senghenydd but, with the couple's agreement, commanded that their wedding presents be put on view at St James' Palace with the admission charge of one shilling (5p). This resulted in a contribution of £1,200 to the

Medical supplies and rescue equipment being unloaded at the pit-head
(courtesy of Mrs E. Prendergast)

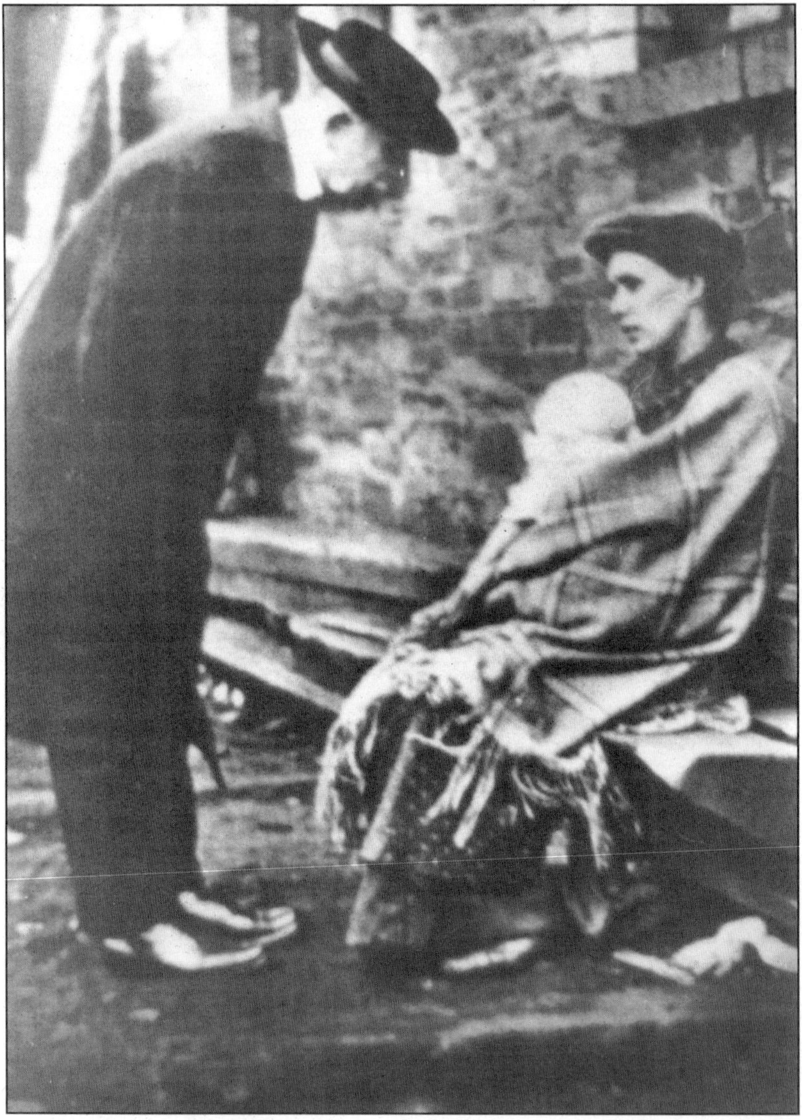

A young wife waiting for news of her husband
is comforted by a local clergyman
(permission of the County of South Glamorgan Libraries)

disaster relief fund — the King himself donated another £500. In his place the King required the Home Secretary, Reginald McKenna, to visit Senghenydd to ascertain the position.

McKenna arrived at Senghenydd just after 7pm that night and was immediately taken to the colliery office. There he met a silent group of grimy men in working clothes smelling of smoke and soot, faces black with coal dust and lined with runnels of sweat. One of them, his grey hair spattered with smuts, stepped forward, with grimy hand outstretched, to greet the Minister with a silent handgrip. Words were superfluous as J. Dyer Lewis, Inspector of Mines for the Western Division, motioned the Home Secretary towards the plan of the mine on the table where Professor Redmayne outlined in low tones the apparently hopeless position for those men still imprisoned in the working places beyond the wall of fire.

Later the Home Secretary inspected the pit-head passing through the waiting crowd silent under the fitful lights around the colliery buildings. His inspection completed he went into Senghenydd to visit and sympathise with the widows and families of men already known to be dead and others still entombed.

By the end of the day the dead numbered fifty-six. Four had died in or on the way to hospital. Fifty had been brought up dead and the remaining two were the decapitated banksman and the rescuer killed by a fall. Four of those recovered were found suffocated in the return road less than thirty yards from the safety of the York shaft. They had come over half a mile from their district to die virtually within sight of safety.

The day ended with some good news. The team of fitters from the Abercynon Colliery under the direction of Leyshon Jenkins had completed the laying of a new column of water pipes down the Lancaster shaft. The column was ready to be connected next morning to the ¾ mile length of pipes being laid to the colliery from the reservoir in the hills above the village.

The day hope was abandoned — Thursday, 16th October

A day destined to be the blackest day for the little valley.

Once again the legal requirements began to be fulfilled with Coroners opening their proceedings to decide the cause of death. At the Gwern y Milwr Hotel in Senghenydd Coroner David Rees took evidence of identification of those brought up dead from the mine and at the Law Courts in Cardiff Coroner W. L. Yorath took similar action in respect of the men who died in hospital at Cardiff. Both inquests were adjourned until later.

The Executive Council of the South Wales Miners Federation also met at the hotel in Senghenydd, passed a vote of sympathy and condolence with the relatives of the dead, and resolved to appeal for funds to relieve distress. They decided to ask the Lord Mayors of London and Cardiff to set up funds for this purpose and also they required the Home Secretary to hold an independent inquiry into the circumstances of the disaster at the colliery.

From the committee of mining experts at the colliery came the shattering news that all exploratory work was suspended. Bad as this sounded, hope finally disappeared when William Brace MP said, quite pointedly, it had to be recognised that all those in the pit had perished. The enormity of this news and the sudden destruction of even forlorn hope left the little valley numb with shock.

What had happened was that the fighting of the fires in the Lancaster Level and in the No. 1 North was not proceeding to the optimistic expectations of the committee of experts and they were having to rethink their approach. Furthermore the fire had effectively blocked the ventilation of the west side of the mine for over two days and it was unlikely that the men in the workings would still be alive.

Days of frustration by fire — Friday to Sunday, 17th to 19th October

The plan now became one of controlling the fire with the ultimate aim of walling it in to complete the dousing and then to restore the ventilation.

On Friday the fire in the No 1 North was conquered by men wearing smoke helmets and supplied with air by flexible tube and bellows. During the day a supply of sandbags and sand was sought to make a 'bashing' or wall at the end of the No 1 North cross-cut west of the fire in the Lancaster Level. The sandbags were filled on the surface, taken below and then transported to the Lancaster Level. There they were laid across the width of the road to a depth of six or seven yards and piled up to the roof. Each layer was jammed tightly together and the joints between the bags rammed tight with turf and earth. The turfs were cut from the mountainsides around the mine by gangs of men who rushed them to the pit-head in trams on a hurriedly constructed tramroad. It was all a massive exercise involving hundreds of men both above and below ground.

Saturday and Sunday saw the valley inundated by a flood of mournful black as the first of the dead were buried. Silent crowds, estimated at 150,000, gathered at the pit-head and lined the streets to pay tribute to eleven men buried on Saturday and eight on Sunday. The cortege on Saturday was over a mile long and was led by Salvation Army bands from Barry, Pentre and Bargoed paying their tribute to two of their soldiers — Colour Sergeant E. Gilbert and Bandsman Emrys Williams.

The face of grief. The worst is known and the grieving wife is escorted home by a Salvation Army lass
('Daily Mirror' photo — permission of Syndication International Ltd)

One of the Universal Colliery's rescue teams. Two of these men — William Hyatt and George Spreadbury — died in the explosion.
(courtesy of Mr David R. Lewis — son of David Lewis in the Rescue Team)

Most of the bodies were for burial in the valley's new cemetery at Penyrheol where provision had already been made for 350 graves for the disaster's victims — an indication of how quickly the future had closed down for this mining community. During the following six weeks the valley was to witness hundreds of funerals with an effect which was to make itself felt for years ahead.

By Sunday night the situation underground at the colliery had improved measurably. The construction of the bashing was still proceeding but already the volume of smoke had been considerably reduced and the temperature was much lower.

Days of cautious exploration — Monday and Tuesday, 20th and 21st October

With the fire subdued in the No 1 North and entry secured into the Lancaster Level exploring parties made cautious forays into the workings on the west side. The experts felt that if there was anyone still alive on that side of the mine it would be only beyond the Mafeking Storage. As the rescue parties pushed out in that direction they encountered heavy falls with a particularly massive one at the Ladysmith Parting east of the Mafeking Storage. By Tuesday night they had retrieved nine more bodies and penetrated into Mafeking and Kimberley Districts — they returned convinced there was no-one alive in either. But now smoke and steam was escaping from the bashing in the main west intake (the Lancaster Level) and this bashing needed to be strengthened if ventilation was to be maintained to allow exploration to continue.

Days of further frustration — Wednesday to Tuesday, 22nd to 28th October

On Wednesday, 22nd October the official statement informed the waiting valley that work was to be directed towards strengthening the main west bashing and inspecting the main west return — and although parties had penetrated into both Mafeking and Kimberley further exploration would be deferred.

Next morning the pit top was deserted — a visible recognition that public interest had died as surely as all those men still unrecovered from the unexplored west side districts.

For the next five days work concentrated on strengthening the Lancaster Level bashing and in erecting a bashing at the stables to improve ventilation on the west side. Ventilation was of paramount importance if exploring parties were to overcome falls and enter districts where gas had accumulated for nearly two weeks.

Days of fumes and falls — Wednesday, 29th October to Tuesday, 17th November

Exploration resumed on Wednesday, 29th October with an attempt to break into Ladysmith. Probing forays had already enabled parties to examine the main points of both entry into, and return from, Ladysmith, Mafeking and Pretoria and these probes had decided the committee of experts to examine Ladysmith first.

The advance into Ladysmith was halted by a large fall and an accumulation of gas in the double parting on the main road into the district. This was to be the pattern for exploring parties in the next three weeks — falls, heart-breaking in size and back-breaking to breach, with dangerous blowers and accumulations of gas.

This first fall was pierced the next day and by Thursday night over 100 tons of debris had been removed and four bodies recovered in the process. A further fall 100 yards long and 30 to 40 feet high was encountered in the Ladysmith Main Level on Saturday, 1st November.

By Thursday, 6th November exploration of the district had brought the total number of bodies recovered to 144 but it was not to be until the morning of Saturday, 8th November that the official statement reported exploration of Ladysmith had been completed and the last six bodies had been brought out. The delay between discovering the dead and bringing their bodies to the surface was due entirely to the work involved in breaching the massive obstructing falls. After the initial entry into workings had been made it was necessary to consolidate the entry to enable working parties to remove the bodies in safety. For this reason the number of bodies recorded as recovered lagged behind those discovered.

With Ladysmith explored and a third of the dead removed, attention turned to Kimberley, Mafeking and Pretoria. No exploration was carried out on Sunday, 9th November but preparations for this task included the erection of a bashing outside the entrance to No 1 North Level to prevent fumes going into the Kimberley Main. This bashing, with that at the No 1 North cross-cut, effectively boxed in the site of the main fire in the Lancaster Level and enabled air for Ladysmith to be directed towards Kimberley and Pretoria. This bashing was completed on Monday morning (10th November).

On Tuesday thirty bodies were found in Pretoria but in all districts the advancing parties were still being held up by the massive falls. In the Mafeking Return a fall of about 200 tons of debris was encountered and this had to be cleared to permit safe passage into the working places.

Kimberley was explored by Thursday, 13th November when twenty-

Members of a rescue party being assisted in the arrangement of their safety helmets before descent
(permission of the Illustrated London News Picture Library)

five bodies were discovered. The toll of those recovered rose to 177 by that night but by now Mafeking had been breached and the way was open into Pretoria.

By Monday, 17th November both Mafeking and Pretoria had yielded up their dead and in the four days from Friday the colliery winding gear raised nearly 200 bodies. They were found in groups of six or seven and even twelve. Many had not had time to collect their coats or lamps. These were found still hanging on nails where they had been left.

This recovery of over 200 bodies over the weekend severely strained the resources of the mortuary team whose task it was to prepare the bodies prior to identification by relatives. After a month underground the bodies were grossly decomposed while many were also badly mutilated. In many cases facial identification was impossible — these bodies were completely wrapped in winding sheets on which personal belongings found on the body were placed, in the hope they would assist recognition. One young boy, badly mutilated and nearly completely unclothed by the explosion, was identified only by a black patch sewed on his singlet and some notches on his boots. Another was recognisable only by the champagne cork in his tea jack which had been given to him by his 'butty' or friend.

The space required for laying out the bodies for identification greatly exceeded that available on the colliery premises and it was as well that arrangements had been made to use the village's St John Ambulance Brigade Hall as a hospital and a mortuary. Known as Aberdare Hall it was situated on the hillside below Stanley Street in Senghenydd. Because of awkward entrance steps bodies were carried into the back of the hall through the adjoining house in No 2 Stanley Street.

On Thursday, 20th November 1913 the Western Mail reported that the total death roll due to the explosion was officially stated to be 439. 406 bodies had been recovered leaving 33 still in the pit. Of the 406 recovered 346 had been identified, six had died after being brought out injured, 48 were still unidentified and six had been buried unknown. Only now were Senghenydd and Abertridwr able to appreciate what the effects of the explosion meant to their communities. * From Senghenydd 301 wage earners had been killed, from Abertridwr and Penyrheol 79, from Caerphilly 32, 24 from elsewhere in the district with eight buried as unknown. Overall 542 children had been left without a father, 205 women had been widowed and 62 parents and other dependants had been deprived of a wage earner's support.

Figures are finite in character and give no indication of the degree of sorrow and grief falling to individual families. They do not reveal that in twelve homes both father and son were killed, in three homes the father and two sons died, that ten families lost two sons and two others each lost three sons.

They do not show that when Edwin John Small died with his 21 year old son, Edwin Samuel Small, it left his 18 year old daughter Mary with the care of six children — the youngest was three years old — in the village of Orcop in Herefordshire. Father and son had left Orcop to lodge and work in Senghenydd after Mrs Small had died twelve months earlier.

Nor do figures show that Mrs Ross of 22 Coronation Terrace, Senghenydd, lost her husband, two sons, a brother, and a lodger, who lived with the family.

This catalogue of death, loss and grief could be extended without remotely accomplishing a complete account of the anguish resulting from an explosion of gas and coal dust in a colliery in a little known Welsh valley.

Those still alive after the explosion had a heightened recognition of the enormity of the disaster and they and their representatives were soon vociferous in their demands to learn what had happened and why — and, equally important, who was to blame.

Time was to show that they were not to be satisfied on any of these scores.

* This reflects a breakdown by locality of the 436 listed as killed in Appendix II — out of the total of 439 killed by the explosion and one rescuer killed by a fall.

Chapter 9

Of Coroners and Commissioners

ANY REASONABLE person would expect the Home Secretary, with the worst disaster in the history of mining in Britain on his hands, to have lost no time in invoking his powers under the 1911 Coal Mines Act to hold an official inquiry into the disaster.

Section 83 of this Act enabled him to hold an investigation into the cause and circumstances of any mining accident. The Act required the investigation to be carried out in open court by a person competent to hold an inquiry. Also — and this was to be a stumbling block — the Horne Secretary could appoint an assessor or assessors to assist the investigating commissioner with his inquiry.

As it was, the Home Office nabobs took over two months to decide to hold an inquiry and to appoint a Commissioner and two Assessors. This delay leads one to infer there was an element of reluctance to make the inquiry as searching as the miners of Great Britain required it should be.

Once the decision to hold the inquiry had been taken and the 'competent persons' had been appointed one would also expect the arrangements for it, and those for the Coroner's inquest, to have gone smoothly. Again this was not to be and the saga of mishap and misfortune attaching to the Universal Colliery was to extend even to these official functions.

The first demand from the miners for a full scale inquiry came from the South Wales Miners' Federation after their meeting in Senghenydd on 16th October 1913. This was followed by a supporting demand seven days later from the Miners' Federation of Great Britain, whose deputation met Home Secretary Reginald McKenna on 27th October to press their claims. This deputation was led by Robert Smillie, their president and accompanied by William Brace MP from Wales. McKenna was sympathetic but wished to consult the coal owners first.

At a further meeting in November McKenna explained that difficulty lay in finding an assessor among the coal owners — possibly due to reluctance among owners to sit in judgement on one of their own. This was completely unacceptable to the miners and their continued pressure eventually brought results.

On 18th December 1913 the Warrant of Appointment was issued naming R. A. S. Redmayne CB, the Chief Inspector of Mines, as Commissioner. The two Assessors were named as Robert Smillie, President of the Miners' Federation of Great Britain, and Evan Williams, Chairman of the South Wales and Monmouthshire Coal Owners' Association.

In the meantime Coroner David Rees had been consulting representatives of the miners, the owners and the Mines Inspectorate to agree a suitable date for the resumed hearing of the inquest. They were not ready initially but, early in December, agreed for a hearing on 5th January 1914. On 12th December Rees notified the Home Office of his intention to recommence inquest proceedings on this January date. This notification was, of course, before the issue of the Warrant of Appointment.

Later in December Redmayne decided to begin his inquiry on 2nd January 1914. When the Home Office informed the Coroner of this they also asked him to adjourn his inquest. David Rees refused and was firm in his resolve not to give way to the inquiry.

Consequently the decision of the Coroner, as the age old direct representative of the Crown, stood. Even so, and possibly to save face, the inquiry opened at the Law Courts in Cardiff on Friday and Saturday, 2nd and 3rd January 1914, and then adjourned to allow the inquest to proceed.

In his opening remarks on the first day of the inquest hearing at the Gwern y Milwr Hotel in Senghenydd on Monday, 5th January 1914, David Rees detailed these happenings leading to the clash of inquest and inquiry. He explained his reasons for maintaining the precedence of the inquest in these words:-

> Gentlemen, this court has criminal jurisdiction. It did seem to me it is a well established principle that nothing should be done to prejudice the minds of those who have to decide whether someone was culpable or not, . . . or make them come to a conclusion before hearing the spoken evidence which is always produced before the Jury. On those grounds I thought it was of the utmost importance that the inquest should precede the inquiry. On maturer consideration, I see no reason to alter this opinion . . . Now, gentlemen, one further word I wish to say, and it is this. A suggestion has been made

> that, because of the inquiry, this inquest should be curtailed as much as possible. I deprecate that suggestion and I somewhat resent it for these reasons. We are inquiring into the death of 439 persons. I think it is due to them and to those who mourn them, that we should sift every fact, every material fact, which should enable us to apportion the blame — if blame there be — and to place it on the proper shoulders. It is, I think, also due to the thousands of working men who are engaged in coal mining, which is a risky occupation, to make the inquiry as searching and exhausting as we possibly can . . . to find out a means of preventing these terrible catastrophes. It is also due . . . to the mine owners and their officials that fair and ample opportunity should be given to them to place before the court all the facts they think necessary in order to get, at your hands if it should happen, exoneration for anything that has been done.

The inquest hearing took eight days, spread over 5th to 14th January with nearly 9,000 questions being put to 50 witnesses. In comparison Redmayne's inquiry resumed on 27th January, and continued for nearly a month probing a similar number of witnesses with nearly 22,000 questions. Altogether it was much more intensive and technically thorough than the inquest.

At the hearings the major representatives for the main interests were:-

- John Sankey KC (later Lord Sankey) and the Hon Trevor Lewis for the mine owners and management
- W. P. Nicholas and W. E. Harvey MP for the Miners' Federation of Great Britain
- William Brace MP and Thomas Richards MP for the South Wales Miners' Federation
- Dr W. N. Atkinson and Colonel Andrew Pearson for the Mines Inspectorate and Home Office
- Clement Edwards MP for a number of the bereaved families

The evidence obtained at both inquest and inquiry overlaps to a large extent and there is more profit in considering the findings of the two hearings rather than sifting through the minutiae of the voluminous evidence they recorded. Both hearings were required to determine the reason for the death of 439 miners — with the inquest detailing the cause of death of each man — and whether anyone was to blame for it. This called for a thorough examination of the management and working of the mine —

including inspection of working places and the control of coal dust.

At May 1913 the seams being worked in the mine were the Four Feet, the Universal and the Nine Feet, all situated between 500 and 560 yards down. Coal was wound mainly from a landing at the Six Feet seam (530 yards down) in both Lancaster and York pits. The workings underground still adhered to the two main divisions of east side and west side.

As the explosion was confined to the west side both inquest and inquiry concentrated on determining the conditions prevailing in the six districts worked on that side of the mine. These were the West York, Pretoria, Mafeking, Kimberley Ladysmith and Bottanic, all of which branched away from the main air intake of the Lancaster Level. (See plan on page 65.)

Ventilation — General

The mine was ventilated by a 24ft diameter Walker type fan which exhausted air from the York shaft and generated an air current of over 200,000ft^3 per minute down the Lancaster shaft. About three quarters of this fed into the west side and the remainder into the east side.

Normally this amount of air should have been adequate to ventilate all the workings on the west side but both inquiries criticised the system of ventilating Kimberley, Mafeking and Pretoria.

Both Redmayne and the Coroner found the west side of Mafeking was ventilated by air which had already circulated in Kimberley — but the Coroner went further and pointed out that this air was then taken into the West York District. He felt air which had already done its work in two districts was not the best for ventilating a third. This did not constitute a breach of ventilation regulations but such breaches were soon to be revealed.

Ventilation — Reversing the Air Current

The most important of these was the inability to reverse the air current. This was a requirement of Section 31(3) of the Coal Mines Act 1911 and operative on 1st January 1913. On application by the colliery company to the South Wales Division Inspector of Mines this date had been extended, for the Senghenydd mine, to 16th September and again to 30th September 1913. On the day of the explosion — fourteen days after the extended expiry date — the work had still not been done and the air current through the mine was not immediately reversible. For the owners and the manager their counsel at the inquiry, Trevor Lewis, frankly admitted this was a breach of the legal requirement.

Inevitably, this failure posed the question whether an immediate reversal would have been the means of saving life. Redmayne and Evan

Williams felt that men in the West York District might have been saved but at the expense of those brought out of the Bottanic District.

Robert Smillie, the other assessor, disagreed most strongly with these findings of his two colleagues. He criticised the Inspectors of Mines for failing to ensure that the work, necessary to effect reversal of the air current, was carried out before the expiry of either of the two extensions they had granted. He felt that the discussions which took place more than once on the afternoon of the day of the explosion decided against reversing the current 'because it was found impossible, as provision . . . (for this) . . . had not been made.'

Smillie couldn't prove it but the whole tenor of his memorandum to Redmayne's report implied he felt reversal would have saved more men on the west side.

Whether it was Redmayne or Smillie who had correctly deduced the possible effects of not reversing the air current it is not now possible to say. The unresolved doubt was whether men had died who might not otherwise have done so if a legal requirement had been met. This was a breach of law for which someone would have to answer.

On the subject of ventilation there were two other matters which gave grounds for adverse comment and were seen as breaches of the Coal Mines Act. One concerned the measurement and recording of the quantity of air entering various parts of the mine, and the other the reading and recording of barometric and hygrometric measurements at the surface and underground, where appropriate.

Ventilation — Measurement of Air Current

The Act, and attendant regulations, required the measurement each month of the quantity of air in the main ventilating current to each seam, in every split in the current (i.e. where an intake road into a district forked off from the main intake road), and at a point 100 yards back from the first working place at the face. These measurements were required to be recorded in a book maintained in the mine for that purpose.

These three sensible requirements were designed to ensure that adequate ventilation was provided throughout the workings and that it was duly recorded.

Inquiries showed that whilst the first two measurements were taken those at 'a point 100 yards back' were not. Shaw contended they were not necessary because there was no leakage of air between the entrance to the split and the working places. Be that as it may, the failure to do so was a breach of legal requirements and Redmayne recorded it as such. Also he

A rescue party leaves the mine after an all-night search
(courtesy of Mrs A. Holder)

Three of the eighteen men rescued form the Bottanic District — George Moore and his two sons, George (left) and Evan James
(courtesy of Mr Evan James Moore)

found the measurements were not recorded in the form required by the Home Office, thereby compounding another breach.

Ventilation — Atmospheric Readings

The overall investigation into all aspects of the ventilation of the mine convinced both inquiries there had also been a failure to measure and record barometric and hygrometric readings.

Atmospheric pressure was an important factor in determining the level of ventilation in any mine where gas was prevalent. A reduction in this pressure could result in abnormal emission of gas from coal seams in workings where it would normally be held back by the pressure of air. This could be counteracted by increasing the fan speed to produce a greater air current and increased ventilation to dilute and diffuse the gas.

For this reason a thermometer and barometer was required to be sited above ground near the entrance to the mine — with a hygrometer, for moisture readings, underground in both the main intake and return airways. All these instruments were to be read daily and recorded. Both inquest and inquiry found readings were taken but not recorded; Shaw admitted this record was not kept.

To satisfy himself there was nothing atmospherically abnormal on the day of the explosion Redmayne obtained barometric readings from the Bute Office at Aberdare — some ten miles away as the crow flies. These confirmed that pressure was comparatively high at 29.8 to 30 inches, so was most unlikely to have had any effect on the events around the explosion. But failure to keep a record was another breach of legal requirements — to add to those relating to ventilation.

Lamps and Lampmen

The only flames lawfully and knowingly taken into the mine were those enclosed in the proven safety of the lamps issued to each worker needing to go underground. Thus it was quite natural for both the inquest and the inquiry — more so the inquiry — to examine in detail both the lamps and their issue.

The oil burning miners' lamps were tended and lit by the lamp attendant at the surface. Before they were issued to the miners the lamps were locked with a lead rivet locking device to prevent their being opened underground by anyone unauthorised to do so.

After the men got underground they were met by their firemen at lamp locking stations — one on the east side and one on the west side — where the lamps were examined prior to the workmen going on to their work places. These lamp stations were situated just off the main intake airway and were manned by attendants known as lamp lockers. Their other function was to provide facilities for relighting the lamp of any man who 'lost his light' when at work and so obviate the need for his return to the surface lamp room to do this.

The examination of these functions showed that the lamps used at the mine had been approved by the Home Secretary but the glasses fitted to the lamps had not been so approved.

Also, the surface lamp room attendant and the lamp lockers — although authorised by Edward Shaw to carry out their duties — had not been appointed in writing as required by Section 34 of the Act.

Both Commissioner and Coroner were at pains to point out the competence of the men was in no way disparaged by this omission. It was a technical breach which had occurred and needed to be recorded as such — but a breach nevertheless.

Management and Supervision

One of the most important aspects of the management of the mine invoking the scrutiny of both inquiries was the examination by firemen of districts and working places.

In his summing-up speech Coroner David Rees vividly described the functions of firemen in these words:-

> If I may use a simile, I think firemen are the scouts who precede the army of workmen into the mine to inspect the places where those workmen are going to during the day, and to come back to a certain spot to tell the workmen whether the enemy is present in the shape of gas or of anything else.

In effect a fireman was required to examine the whole area underground for which he was responsible to ensure that it was safe for the workmen to work there. This was a legacy from the early days of coal mining when men were sent in to the workings to 'fire' any accumulated gas before other workers went in. These men were armed with long poles with lighted flares or tapers attached. Crawling into workings in the prone position they would cautiously raise the flare to the roof to burn off the gas there. Many times this resulted in explosions, but more often the gas would burn off harmlessly above the prone firemen. To protect themselves from burns these old firemen wrapped themselves in rags and old clothes soaked in water — for this reason their beggar-like appearance also earned them the title of 'penitents' but it was the term 'fireman' which ultimately stuck and survived. On the day shift — the coal producing shift — the times of descent and ascent of the firemen and colliers etc were as follows:-

	Descent	*Ascent*
Day firemen	3:30am	1pm
Colliers and others	5:10 – 6am	2pm

Coal raising was carried out from 6am to 2pm

This arrangement enabled the day firemen to comply with the legal provisions requiring inspection of the workings to 'be commenced and completed within the two hours immediately preceding the commencement of work in the district.'

In effect, during these two hours the firemen had to descend the pit, walk into their districts, examine all the roads and working places for safety and then return to an appointed meeting place to meet incoming workmen in order to inform them of gas, danger etc. In most collieries in Britain a meeting place was normally provided in each district but at Senghenydd there was but one for the whole of the west side. This was at the lamp locking station on the Lancaster Level some 440 yards from the bottom of the Lancaster shaft.

The question immediately presenting itself to both inquiries was whether the firemen were able to do all required of them within the two hours at their disposal. To satisfy himself on this point Redmayne obtained details of the distances each fireman had to walk and the number of working places and men for whose safety he was responsible. He found most of them had to walk a mile to the first working place and all of them had to complete a circuit varying from two to over three miles. Working places ranged between 11 with 31 workmen, to 46 with 125 workmen.

Redmayne felt some of the firemen were hard pressed to get around their districts and get back to the lamp station in the time. Nevertheless, if there had been a meeting place in each district he thought the districts would not have been too large to allow thorough inspection before work commenced. However, Robert Smillie was convinced that all the firemen's districts were too large and would still be so if the meeting places were moved nearer to the working faces. Evan Williams rejected any contention that the districts were too large. He stoutly defended Shaw's claim that a single lamp station and meeting place enabled overmen and firemen to meet and learn the condition of all districts and so decide on any conditions calling for attention or urgent action.

The inquest jury did not comment on this point.

The air of doubt surrounding this safety function did not constitute any contravention of legal requirements.

Incidence of Gas and Testing

Both Redmayne and Coroner David Rees criticised the method used by the firemen for testing for gas in cavities in the roof underground.

The presence of gas anywhere was demonstrated by a lengthening of the flame in a miner's lamp, with the extent of the increase in the length of the flame indicating the concentration of gas present. The correct procedure required a fireman to lower the flame in his lamp, ascend into the roof cavity where gas was suspected to have collected, and observe the extension of the flame to deduce the concentration.

Instead, firemen raised their lamps, with lowered flames, into cavities at the end of a stick about five feet long. Both inquiries recorded the visual difficulty of detecting and assessing the lengthening of a flame in the lamp at the end of a stick, often held at arm's length above the observing fireman's head.

Redmayne was astonished to learn this method was practised at many other South Wales mines. His reaction to this slack method of testing for gas in South Wales collieries noted for their gassy and fiery nature was understandable. It was even more pertinent to the Senghenydd mine with its history of a major explosion in 1901, a massive outburst of gas which stopped work in 1910, and as a mine which generated about 1,200ft^3 of gas per minute — a reading taken by Mines Inspector J. M. Carey just two weeks before the explosion. This reading was not exceptional but it was indicative of the continued presence of gas in the mine.

It was all evidence which incited William Brace MP to press Edward Shaw at the inquest to admit that the mine was a deadly and dangerous one — and worse than usual in respect of gas and coal dust. Shaw refused to concede this point.

The Coroner concluded it was 'what we may call an average gassy mine' but Redmayne said the 1,200ft^3 reading was 'typical of the more *fiery* mines in the steam coal area of the South Wales coal field.'

Both inquiries were concerned with these aspects of gas detection in the course of their examination of evidence to deduce where the explosion started.

Presence of Coal Dust

The investigations, by both inquiries, into the prevention and control of coal dust were directed at the provisions of Section 62 of the Act. Examination concentrated on the loss of coal dust from trams, the watering of coal in transit in the trams, the watering of roadways and the clearance of dust from the floor, roof and sides of roads.

Seven of the eighteen men and boys rescued from the Bottanic District.
Back row: Wilf Vizard, Archibald Dean.
Centre row: Ernest Jones, Ben David, George Moore Snr.
Front row: Evan James Moore, Matron (Porthcawl Miners' Rest), George Moore Jnr. *(courtesy of Mr Evan James Moore)*

Bodies of victims are taken from the pit to the mortuary
(permission of the National Museum of Wales)

Trams

Within five years from 16th December 1911 all waggons in use in coal mines were required, under the Act, to be dust-tight in sides, ends and floors. The management of the mine were gradually bringing about this replacement and at the time of the explosion had already replaced a few hundred trams with those closed on all sides.

This was not enough for William Brace MP who, at the inquest, led Shaw to agree that dust-tight trams would have prevented much of the coal dust in the mine — and then berated him for not having all dust-tight trams in a highly dangerous colliery.

In reply Shaw said:-

> I do not think it is quite fair to ask me why I should do what no other man in the coal field has done. You are asking me to do what no-one else has done to my knowledge.

Touche — and a point to Shaw. Legally he was not required to replace any trams until November 1916 and there had been no offence in law. From the outset it was a fruitless pursuit by Brace.

Control and Clearing of Dust

The clearance from roads of the dust, which had accumulated there due to the haulage of coal on the day shift, was carried out during the afternoon and night shifts. Eight men were detailed to do this by shovelling up the dust from the floor of the roads and removing it to the surface in trams. The eight men worked in pairs but they found it physically impossible to clear every twenty-four hours the whole length of the roads assigned to them.

Shaw admitted he had not found a satisfactory method of clearing the dust from the roof and sides. He had tried removing it with brushes and blowing it away with compressed air, but both methods had merely disturbed the dust causing it to lodge on other timbers. Spraying the roof and sides with water had rarely proved to be effective and then only where the timbering was close together. In other places Shaw said the water softened the walls and roof causing them to collapse under the 'squeeze' i.e. pressure.

From pit bottom in to the districts on the west side coal dust was laid by hoses fed from the water pipes laid along the roads. Where these pipes terminated they fed sprinklers fixed in the roof; these watered the loaded waggons as they passed underneath. From the end of the pipes in towards the working faces water was spread from tanks drawn by horses. As the tank was drawn along the plug was removed and the outflowing water distributed by shovels and buckets.

This examination of the system of dust control led Redmayne to conclude that the siting of the sprinklers was largely ineffective; they were not placed where the haulage of trams commenced and, consequently, would not prevent a great deal of dust being formed.

However, both inquiries were convinced that the watering of the floors of roads had been adequate but the watering and clearing of dust from sides and roofs had been tried and then neglected, rather than rejected.

Counsel for Shaw and the owners realised the implications of this latter point and, in defence, advanced his own interpretation of Section 62(3) of the Act. (This required 'the floor, roof and sides of the road shall be systematically cleared so as to prevent, as far as practicable, coal dust accumulating.') He argued this meant the clearing of dust from floor, roof and sides should be carried out as far as practicable.

Evan Williams, in his report, agreed with this interpretation but Redmayne rejected both. He interpreted the section as requiring the systematic clearing of floor, roof and sides and that the words 'as far as practicable' related to the prevention of the accumulation of coal dust.

The last word remains with Redmayne in a sentence from each of paragraphs 27 and 123 of his report:-

> § 27 — . . . From my inspection of the mine, subsequent to the explosion, I have no doubt whatever that coal dust existed on the roof, sides and timber in dangerous quantity.
>
> § 123 — As no attempt had been made for a long time to clear the roof and sides of coal dust, a breach of Section 62(3) of the Act seems clearly to have been committed.

It seems clear, also, that the lessons preached by Professor Galloway before and after the 1901 explosion at Senghenydd, coupled with the harsh experience of Courrieres, had been heeded in part only.

The Electrical Signalling System

The remaining major aspect of the operation of the Senghenydd mine calling for examination was that of the functioning of the electrical signalling system used underground. It was a subject to exercise both inquest and inquiry for a large part of the time they heard evidence.

There were more than a dozen sets of signalling apparatus in the main intake and haulage roads of the mine but it was the set in the Mafeking Hard Heading (or Incline as it was sometimes called) that was to attract particular attention as a possible source of the explosion.

(A 'Hard Heading' was a road, sometimes inclined, driven through rock strata to connect different workings, or different levels of workings, in a mine to provide for access and for haulage of trams, coal and supplies etc.)

The main components of the signalling apparatus were a bell, a battery and a pair of bare wires. The electric bell was of the trembler type and was protected by a cast iron cover which was not gas tight. The battery comprised six to nine dry cells of the 'Dania' type with each cell producing about 1½ volts when new. The bells and batteries were generally fixed in the engine houses in the haulage roads they served, with the wires of the circuit being laid 12 to 18 inches apart along one side of the road. To ring the bell and provide a signal to the engineman the circuit could be completed either by bringing the wires together or by bridging them with a knife or file.

Every time the circuit was broken, by releasing the wires or removing the bridging contact, sparks appeared at the instant of break. Similarly when the bell rang a succession of sparks formed at the make and break contacts under the iron cover.

In a mine, like that at Senghenydd, where gas was likely to occur in dangerous quantities, the regulations required the electrical signalling apparatus to be so made, installed, serviced and operated so that there was 'no risk of open sparking.' 'Open sparking' carried a deeper meaning than that of a spark capable of being seen; it was a spark capable of igniting inflammable gas outside the apparatus.

In effect the question engaging both inquiries was whether the sparks generated by the signalling systems at Senghenydd were capable of igniting an explosive mixture of firedamp and air in the mine. This question called for an examination of the signalling components and the operation of them under test in explosive mixtures of firedamp.

The maintenance of the signalling apparatus was the responsibility of H. W. Schielbach, the consulting electrical engineer of the Lewis Merthyr Consolidated Collieries Ltd., but regular inspection was carried out by Charles Waddon senior and his son Charles junior. Waddon senior was responsible to the colliery management for the proper performance of the apparatus but his son did most of the actual inspection.

(To appreciate the electrical evidence presented at the inquiries it is sufficient to differentiate between volts (pressure) and amps (current). In a simple analogy if one compares water being forced along a pipe to electric current in a wire then the pressure (the voltage — provided by a battery) is the force pushing the amount of water (the amount of electric current — measured by the number of amps, or amperage) through the pipe (the wire).)

In their evidence about the two sets of signalling apparatus in the Mafeking Hard Heading the Waddons said, and Schielbach confirmed their statement:- that both batteries serving the sets had never recorded readings more than nine volts. (They were capable of producing 13½ and 12 volts respectively.)

Redmayne found that the measurements taken by the Waddons were made on a linesman's detector which needed considerable care to obtain an accurate reading. Also he found the voltage of the cells diminished after use and recovered almost to its former value in a few hours if left unused. (This recovery propensity of the Dania cell was confirmed by its makers.) On this basis Redmayne concluded it was possible for the batteries in the mine to exceed 9 volts, particularly early in the morning and after week-ends.

To ascertain whether the Senghenydd apparatus was capable of igniting an explosive mixture of gas and air Robert Nelson, the Electrical Inspector of Mines, carried out a series of tests at the New Tredegar Rescue Station. He found that explosion of the mixture did not take place where the voltage was below 13½. Evidently the batteries in the Mafeking Hard Heading were unlikely to produce a voltage approaching this level — and Redmayne could not have been faulted if he had accepted these results at face value. However, he was not satisfied that the tests were sufficiently exhaustive and sought 'further evidence from the Home Office's experimental station.'

The tests there were carried out by Dr R. V. Wheeler using bells and cells of the make and size in use at Senghenydd at the time of the explosion. The results of the tests were surprising.

Dr Wheeler's experiments showed that the strength (or amperage) of the current was of more importance than the pressure (or voltage) — and that explosion was more likely when the amount of gas, in the gas and air mixture, was between 5.6% and 14.8%. His tests proved that 'with three Dania cells giving a current . . . of 0.45 amperes under a pressure . . . of 4.5 volts it is possible to produce a spark to explode a mixture of air and methane when methane is present to the extent of 8.2%.' This showed that the explosion would have originated in electrical sparking.

There had been no breach of law by the colliery management but they could be criticised on the basis that they failed to recognise the existence of a risk. Redmayne's comment was:- 'It is all the more astonishing that the management should have faced the risks that the sparks produced might have ignited gas in view of the Bedwas Colliery explosion, which occurred on 27th March 1912, and which was proved beyond reasonable doubt to have been caused by the sparks from an electric bell.' Redmayne went on to point out that this danger had been the subject of the circular letter from the Inspector of Mines to all owners of mines throughout South Wales. Ignorance could not be a justifiable plea.

But in his report Evan Williams repudiated the contention that the signalling installations were capable of producing a spark which would ignite a methane and air mixture. This opinion was based mainly on the tests carried out by Nelson at New Tredegar — although he did recommend the Government to carry out exhaustive experiments to determine what signalling apparatus was appropriate for use in mines liable to outbursts of gas. Also he concluded from his observations in the Mafeking Hard Heading that the explosions had not originated from the signalling system there. He felt the positions of the journeys at the top and bottom of the incline indicated that no signalling could have been going on when the explosion occurred.

Evan Williams was entitled to his opinion that the explosion did not and could not originate in a spark from the signalling system but the weight of evidence, coupled with the Bedwas Colliery experience, justified its consideration as a possibility. Both the inquest and inquiry recognised this and paid it due attention in arriving at their conclusion about the source and seat of the explosion.

The origin and cause of the explosion

With all the evidence duly presented the final act required of both hearings was to determine, to the best of their ability, how and where the explosion originated. It would have been an incongruity in this baleful saga if both conclusions had been similar.

Both hearings examined the question of gas being ignited initially by one or more of four possible sources. These were a naked light from a lamp or match; a fall, with sparks from the falling rock igniting gas; friction of haulage ropes on sheaves (i.e. rollers) or on timber causing sparks or flame; and the sparks from the signalling system. Shot firing was ruled out as no shots had been fired in the mine since Sunday, 12th October.

It was most unlikely the safety precautions would have allowed a miner to get into the workings with matches in his pockets and there was nothing to support a supposition that the explosion had originated in this way. Thus, matches were discarded as a possibility; but the same could not be said about miners' lamps.

After an explosion in a coal mine many broken lamps are to be found in the area affected by the blast from the explosion. As the Coroner said in his summing-up speech when dealing with this subject: 'If the explosion is of sufficient force to blow a beam weighing 500 lb from its original position I do not suppose that a lamp could withstand anything of the kind and I would have expected that a large number of broken lamps would be found about the colliery as a result of the explosion.' In these circumstances a broken lamp of itself could not be taken as firm evidence of the source of the explosion. It needed to be considered in its situation and the conditions of the area surrounding it before any surmise about it as a detonator could be accepted or rejected. In applying these criteria two of the many broken lamps found in the mine merited further consideration — one in the Mafikeng District and one in the lamp station in the Lancaster Level.

The second possibility of a haulage rope causing sparks by friction on a sheave or on timber did not attract a great deal of support and was discounted by both Redmayne and the Coroner.

This left open lamps and sparks, from falls and the signalling apparatus, for consideration as possible flash points for the explosion.

The point of origin attracted two main streams of opinion which put it at two widely separated points in the mine. One placed it in the Lancaster Level somewhere between the end of the No 1 North road and the end of the No 2 South road. The other was somewhere on the Mafeking Hard Heading. Support for the first site came from Edward Shaw and other mining engineers representing management, together with representatives of the workmen. The Mafeking Hard Heading site found support from a number of the Inspectors of Mines and Redmayne himself.

Shaw's theory was that a heavy fall took place about 20 to 30 yards beyond the entrance to the No 1 North road and this released gas which was ignited by sparks caused by the falling rocks. His other possibilities were that the gas was blown towards the lamp station and was ignited by an open lamp there, or it went even further and was exploded by the lamp found in the Mafeking Storage.

Redmayne was not convinced by the supposition in this theory that the heavy fall in the Lancaster Level had occurred before the explosion took place. He argued such a fall would have partially blocked the airway and affected the speed of the fan; the fanman, Benjamin Price, had not observed such a variation in speed. Furthermore, when fire fighters got to the fall they found fire and burning timber beneath the fallen ground — this was an indication of the roof collapsing on to the fire. This made it difficult, if not impossible, to account for timber being ignited after the fall. Other pointers against this theory were that the fire did not spread further into the mine beyond the fall and that the fall, if it had happened before the

An undertaker — thought to be D. C. Jones of Senghenydd — and his men prepare coffins
('Daily Sketch' photo — permission of Thomson Regional Newspapers Ltd)

Turf being cut from the mountainside above the colliery to provide material for the 'bashing' (or wall) to contain the fire. *('Western Mail' photo)*

explosion, should have blocked the ensuing blast and prevented it reaching the Lancaster shaft. This had not happened as evidenced in the wreckage in and around the shaft. He was, in consequence, forced to conclude the fall in the Lancaster Level had happened after the explosion.

The question whether an open lamp in the lamp station caused the explosion exercised the attention of both inquest and inquiry — with widely divergent decisions resulting.

The lamp station attracted interest because of what had been found there. This interest was concentrated on the lamps rather than the bodies of Edward Matthews, the lamp locker, and David Evans, master haulier. On the small table in the station the top of a lamp was found lying on its side. A few inches away was the pot of the lamp — that is the lower half of the lamp containing the oil and wick. The pot of another lamp was found on the floor of the station. Inside the lamp on the table was a piece of paper.

On this evidence was built the theory that David Evans had called at the lamp station to relight his lamp. The lamp had been opened and taken apart for cleaning preparatory to lamp locker Edward Matthews opening his lamp to transfer the flame. When the naked flame was in process of transfer, gas, released by a fall, had swept into the lamp station and exploded.

This was the theory accepted by the inquest jury and acknowledged as the most likely probability by Evan Williams, the assessor.

Redmayne, supported by Robert Smillie, the other assessor, did not subscribe to this, citing the facts that the paper in the lamp at the lamp station was not even scorched. Also, as they pointed out, the recently whitewashed lamp station itself was 'so discoloured as to present the appearance of having been swept by an explosive blast carrying coal dust and smoke . . . if an explosion of gas had originated in the cabin one would not have expected discolouration.' In this context Redmayne's experience was that indications of the development of great force were not to be found at the originating point of colliery explosions; in and around the lamp station the effects of the blasting power of the explosion were all too evident.

For these reasons Redmayne's attention was directed elsewhere. In looking elsewhere he acknowledged that indications of force were an uncertain guide in locating the originating point of an explosion. In fact in some parts of the mine this evidence was conflicting and liable to be interpreted differently by different persons. For these reasons he said he preferred to base his opinion on the evidence of his own eyes. This led him to Mafeking District. As it was, both hearings spent some time considering the conditions before the explosion in a small area in the Mafeking District. Redmayne saw the ground there was faulted and conditions, therefore, were favourable to the production of gas. The bodies of the overman, W. Evans, and the day shift fireman, Ben Davies, were found in this area, although their lamps were about 40 yards away. It transpired that on the morning of the explosion they had spoken to the night overman about conditions in these workings and had gone there because they were anxious about the state of the place.

In fact there was a record, over nearly three weeks, of gas being found and reported in the area. Some of the workmen were worried about this and were convinced that something was bound to happen unless they were very careful. Fred Williams, the fireman, was equally concerned and had told them to be careful with their lamps in the area every morning. Evidence of this was given by a collier named William Thornton who said that, when he discussed the gas with Fred Williams, the fireman had told them to disperse it 'by brushing it away with their coats.' He knew this was a breach of the regulations but was adamant this was what they had been told to do to improve ventilation.

That there was something wrong in these workings was confirmed by the fact that for some days before the explosion Richard Williams of 28 Stanley Street, Senghenydd (known locally and referred to in both hearings as 'Good boy Dick'), had been detailed to drive through between two stall roads to improve the ventilation and disperse the gas.

Neither Redmayne nor the Coroner were convinced the explosion happened in this area but they were obliged to examine the possibility whether a large escape of gas could have originated there and travelled into the return which ended at the Mafeking Storage and been ignited there. Both decided against this.

However, the examination of Good boy Dick's movements and the area in which he worked revealed a possible link between that area and the lamps in the lamp station. It was suggested that one of the two lamps found near where Good boy Dick was working was that of master haulier David Evans — whose body was found in the lamp station. At the inquest Thomas Richards MP, when questioning Edward Shaw, suggested that the lamp of either the fireman or overman could have been extinguished — either by gas in the area or by some other means — and the official had exchanged lamps with master haulier David Evans. Evans had then made his way back to the lamp station for a relight. Shaw agreed such an exchange of lamps was possible but he had no knowledge whether one of the two lamps found in Mafeking was the one originally issued from the surface lamp room to David Evans.

This was not resolved and what transpired was even stranger. William Morse, the lamp man, gave evidence of the issue of lamp No 21 to Edward Matthews, the attendant at the lamp locking station. The two lamps found in the lamp station were numbers 1392 and 4 — recorded as issued to William Owen Williams and Gwilym Williams respectively. Lamp 21, the lamp providing the source for relighting other lamps, was never found.

The enquiries about these lamps, the evidence of gas, the ventilation and the actions of Good boy Dick all raised questions which could not be resolved. All the examination did was to confirm for Redmayne that conditions in parts of the Mafeking District gave cause for concern before and on the day of the explosion.

In the light of the evidence taken from witnesses, the opinions of the mining engineers and mines inspectors, and the evidence of the direction of blast he had seen during his many forays into the mine after the explosion, Redmayne concluded there was 'a strong probability of the explosion having originated on the Mafeking Incline' (or Mafeking Hard Heading).

Very large falls were found in this heading and above the falls large areas of the roof and walls had been blackened by a film of sooty dust deposited by the explosion. This evidence supported Redmayne's postulation that the explosion was preceded by an occurrence similar to that in October 1910 when heavy falls released a massive outburst of gas and closed the pit. The falls in the hard heading exposed seams of coal and beds of rock and he supposed that gas may have come away from these. Ignition of the gas could have been caused either by sparks from falling rocks or from the signalling system, previous explosions were known to have been originated by these causes.

Redmayne formed this opinion about the site of origin and probable cause of the explosion on what he had observed and the evidence he had taken from mining engineers and inspectors. He knew full well it was at variance with the findings of the Coroner's inquest. On 14th January 1914 the jury had answered the nine questions put to them by the Coroner. These were:-

Question 1: Do you find that the 420 persons who met their death at the Universal Colliery on 14th October 1913 died from the causes mentioned by Dr James?

Answer: Yes.

Question 2: Was the colliery properly ventilated on the 14th October 1913?

Answer: Yes.

Question 3: Was the colliery properly inspected on the morning of 14th

October 1913 and was there a sufficient number of examiners employed?

Answer: Yes.

Question 4: Was the explosion caused by gas or coal dust, or by both?

Answer: The explosion was caused by gas and fed by coal dust.

Question 5: Were the floor, roof and sides of the roads systematically cleared so as to prevent, as far as practicable, coal dust accumulating?

Answer: Yes, so far as the floor is concerned, but we are of opinion that more attention should be given to the clearing of the roof and sides, whilst at the same time appreciating the great difficulties of performing the latter. We would suggest, also, the placing of sprinklers much nearer to the working faces than they are at present. Also, that the Home Office be urged to use all its endeavours to find means to effectually deal with the dust problem.

Question 6: Was the gas ignited by electric signalling, either by sparks at the wires, or at the signalling bells, or by sparks from the sheaves, or by a broken lamp, or by a naked light, or how?

Answer: There is insufficient evidence, but we think the weight of evidence points to the naked light at the lamp station.

Question 7: Where did the explosion originate?

Answer: There is insufficient evidence to answer definitely; but the preponderance of evidence points to the lamp station as the probable vicinity where it originated.

Question 8: Did the neglect of any person or persons cause or contribute to the death of the deceased persons?

Answer: No.

Question 9: If not, do you find that death was due to accident?

Answer: Yes; accidental death.

These were the unanimous decisions of all the members of the jury who went further and added their recommendations:-

(a) That the lamp station should be placed in the arch-work near the shaft.

(b) That the water tanks should be fitted with a spray to do away with the necessity of men using shovels and buckets to spray the water.

(c) We are of opinion that there are not sufficient Inspectors of Mines to enable a thorough inspection of the collieries to be made, and as often as the work ought to be done.

So the two inquiries had come up with different answers to the same questions. The inquest jury, voicing the opinions of the mining engineers and Evan Williams, saw the probable point of origin at the lamp station and the flash point the flame of an open lamp. Redmayne, Smillie, and many mines inspectors plumped for the Mafeking Hard Heading with ignition from 'sparks from the electric signalling apparatus or from rocks brought down from the fall.'

It would have been all so very neat and tidy if the findings of both inquiry and inquest had been identical but here again the happenings of 1913 were reflecting those of 1901 by not providing firm answers to the questions of source and cause. The inquiry was undoubtedly more extensive and technically thorough than the inquest and for that reason Redmayne's conclusions can be argued as carrying the greater weight.

Be that as it may, it could also be contended that even the inquiry was not fully comprehensive inasmuch as no director of the colliery company had been called to give evidence. Clement Edwards MP, acting for some of the bereaved families, seized on this point in the closing days of the inquiry when he asked why no-one from the Board of Directors had given evidence 'to show that they took reasonable steps, as proprietors of this colliery, to see that the Act was not broken, there were no breaches of the Act, and that there was no non-compliance with the Act or with the Regulations.'

The reply from the company's legal representative was the directors had no practical knowledge of the working of the mine and the calling of Lord Merthyr or any other director would have wasted the inquiry's time. In view of Lord Merthyr's technical knowledge and mining experience, plus his presence at the mine from the day of the explosion, one is entitled to doubt whether his evidence would have been a waste of time. Or was it that Edward Shaw was deliberately isolated so as to shoulder any or all the blame?

Whatever was the intention there is no doubt that both the inquest and the inquiry revealed and acknowledged the courage displayed by Shaw in the days following the explosion.

Coroner David Rees, at the end of his summing-up speech, had this to say about the rescuers in general and Edward Shaw in particular:-

> I do wish to associate myself with the remarks of Mr Thomas Richards MP, and I do not think I can express it in better language than that of Mr Richards: 'I think the heroic efforts made on that day to save life at this colliery — including that done in the Bottanic — will rank as among the best of any-

> thing that has happened among the many noble records of our past in South Wales.' We can associate Mr Shaw's name very prominently for the very great courage he displayed on that occasion and indeed to all the workmen who were called upon to do rescue work. I think we can safely say that none of them was found wanting.'

In the penultimate paragraph (§137) of his report Commissioner Redmayne wrote:-

> It would be invidious, where all the mining engineers and miners engaged in attempted rescue operations worked so hard in endeavouring to get past the fire into the workings with the object of saving life, to commend individuals by name, but I think a particular meed of praise is due to Mr Shaw and to the small band of workers who accompanied him underground immediately after the explosion.

These acknowledgements of Edward Shaw's courage during the rescue attempts were well and truly deserved — but to whom was blame to be apportioned for all the breaches of the Coal Mines Act revealed during the inquiry? Time was to show that the penalty of the law was not always in proportion to attributable blame.

One of the many funerals passing through the centre of Senghenydd
(permission of the National Museum of Wales)

The Universal Huts — known as 'The Huts' — opposite the colliery at Senghenydd
(permission of the County of South Glamorgan Libraries)

Chapter 10

'Men came cheap . . .'

THE BREACHES of the Coal Mines Act 1911, uncovered by the official inquiry, had alerted the whole mining community who waited to see whether the infringements would result in legal action against the owners and management. As the weeks passed after the end of the inquiry on 21st February 1914, and the official report of the findings had not been published, this expectancy turned to militant concern and action. The South Wales Miners' Federation were moved to bring to the notice of the Home Secretary the delay in publishing the report. At the same time they urged him to start legal proceedings for the breaches and to do this before the six months time limit for prosecution ended on 14th April 1914.

The Coal Mines Act of 1911 was the culmination of the years of work of the Royal Commission of 1906 and embodied the knowledge and experience — often bitter — of miners, the mines inspectorate and owners over many years. It was a serious attempt to set standards for safety and conditions in an industry with a long history of danger, sudden death and disaster. Consequently, the provisions of the Act were quite positive in their protection of the workers from these inherent dangers — but they recognised also that these aims would not be achieved on a voluntary basis. For this reason the Act spelt out the penalties attending failure to comply with its many requirements. Most of its sections detailing these requirements and functions warned that 'Any person employed in or about a mine . . .' or 'Every owner, agent, or manager of a mine . . . who fails to comply with this section shall be guilty of an offence against this Act.'

These provisions laid the way for charges to be brought against Edward Shaw, as manager and agent, and against the Lewis Merthyr Consolidated Collieries Ltd, as the owners, for the breaches revealed by the inquiry.

Early in April 1914 the Home Office acted. On behalf of the Secretary of

State, information was laid concerning the breaches by Dr W. N. Atkinson, H. M. Inspector of Mines for the South Wales Division. His information resulted in seventeen charges against Shaw and four against the company.

The charges were first heard at the Magistrates Court for Caerphilly Lower on 5th May 1914 before E. W. M. Corbett (Chairman) and D. Prosser. None of the parties summoned was present nor were they represented.

The charges against Edward Shaw, with the appropriate legal provisions were:-

1. Neglecting to appoint a person to examine safety lamps at the surface.
2. Neglecting to appoint a person to unlock safety lamps at the lamp station.
   (Charges 1 & 2 — Contrary to Section 34(1) (i) and (ii) of the Coal Mines Act.)
3. Neglecting to appoint an electrician.
   (Contrary to the Special Rules for the use of Electricity in Mines.)
4. Neglecting to enter in a book readings of barometer, thermometer and hygrometer.
5. Failing to cause readings of barometer, thermometer and hygrometer to be entered in a book.
6. Failing to provide a book for entering readings of barometer, thermometer and hygrometer.
   (Charges 4, 5 & 6 — Section 71(2) of the Act.)
7. Failing to provide means of reversing the air current in the mine.
   (Section 31(3) of the Act.)
8. Failing to clear floor, roof and sides of roads to prevent dust accumulating.
9. Failing to cause to be cleared the floor, roof and sides to prevent dust accumulating.
   (Charges 8 & 9 — Section 62(3) of the Act.)
10. Failing to report conditions as to coal dust on the roads and on steps taken to mitigate danger.
11. Failing to cause to be made a report on conditions as to coal dust on the roads and on steps taken to mitigate danger.
    (Charges 10 & 11 — Section 62(5) of the Act.)
12. Neglecting to enter in prescribed book measurements of the quantity of air in the main current and other parts of the mine.
13. Failing to cause to be entered in the prescribed book measurements of the quantity of air in the main current and in other parts of the mine.

(Charges 12 & 13 — Section 29(2) of the Act. General Regulation 77.)

14. Failing to provide a book for the monthly entry of the measurements of the quantity of air in the main current and other parts of the mine.
(Section 24(1) and (2) of the Act.)
15. Allowing safety lamps of a non-approved type to be used in the mine. *(Section 33 of the Act.)*
16. Failing to measure the quantity of air in the main current and in every split and at places set forth in General Regulation 77.
17. Failing to cause to be measured the quantity of air in the main current and in every split and at places set forth in General Regulation 77.
(Charges 16 & 17 — Section 29(2) of the Act. General Regulation 77.)

Those against the colliery company were four of the charges levelled against Edward Shaw — namely 4, 7, 14 and 15. These concerned the failure to record atmospheric readings, failure to provide for reversal of the air current, failure to provide a book for air current readings and the use of safety lamps which were not of an approved type.

The magistrates decided at the hearing on 5th May 1914 to adjourn *sine die.*

The adjourned hearing was resumed at Caerphilly on 17th June 1914 when the magistrates' bench comprised W. W. Ware, Chairman, supported by D. Prosser and C. F. Forestier-Walker.

The prosecution was conducted by Ivor Bowen KC, assisted by Albert Parsons and Clement Edwards MP; for the defence Charles Kenshole represented both the colliery company and Edward Shaw.

A watching brief for the South Wales Miners' Federation was held by W. P. Nicholas; also present for this purpose were William Brace MP, James Winstone and Tom Richards MP. The nature of the charges and the personalities engaged in arguing them ensured that the trial of the company and Shaw would result in a repetition of the evidence produced at the inquest and inquiry. It could be argued that the passage of time between inquiry and court hearing allowed some evidence to be embroidered or, more kindly, presented afresh; the reader must judge.

In the minds of the miners and their representatives there was no doubt that the infractions of the Act had all been established by Redmayne. All that remained to be determined were the penalties to be inflicted. Realisation was destined not to measure up to expectation.

The first charge taken against Shaw was that of his failure to appoint in writing the surface lamp room attendant. Early in the process of taking this evidence the magistrates decided they would reserve their decision on all charges until all the evidence had been heard. This was to result in the trial continuing into the second half of July 1914 by which time public attention was diverted to the war clouds gathering over Europe.

In his defence of the appointment of lamp room attendant, William Morse, Charles Kenshole pointed out Morse had filled this post most competently for 17½ years. When he was first employed by the Universal Steam Coal Company Morse had been given a note by the manager for the purpose of being registered in the company's books. This was repeated in 1905 when the Lewis Merthyr Consolidated Collieries assimilated the Universal Colliery. Kenshole contended this constituted compliance with the requirements of the Act. However, when Morse was cross-examined and pressed for details of the appointment notes he admitted that the employment had been described as 'lamp room' rather than 'lamp man.'

In response to the similar charge about the appointment of the lamp locker at the underground lamp station Kenshole admitted there had been a technical breach of the legal requirements — but this in no way reflected on the competency of the lamp man concerned.

Evidence covering the appointment of an electrician was produced by H. W. Schielbach, the electrical engineer to the colliery company. He showed the court a book proving that on 18th July 1913 he had forwarded all the necessary forms required under the Act. The forms included one covering the appointment of Charles Waddon as electrician at the colliery.

The bench then decided they would take together all the charges affecting the recording of the readings of the barometer, thermometer and hygrometer. For the company and the manager, Kenshole admitted a book had not been provided for this purpose and, consequently, no entries could have been made.

The seventh charge against Shaw and the second against the company was that of failure to provide means of reversing the air current. In pressing this charge Ivor Bowen stressed that this was a most serious breach of requirements; in this attitude he was reflecting the feelings of Professor Redmayne, Robert Smillie, and the Mines Inspectorate. He reiterated the Act's requirement that provision for this should have been made by 1st January 1913, that no action had been taken until April 1913 when an extension had been sought, and that action had still not been taken when the second extension expired on 30th September 1913.

Kenshole admitted this omission constituted a breach of the Act but

Shaw disputed this. When Dr W. N. Atkinson, Mines Inspector, had been cross-examined on this subject at the inquiry he had advanced the information that reversal could have been effected by making an opening in a wall. Shaw argued this implied reversal of the air current could have been carried out fairly quickly. Thus, the charge depended on the interpretation of 'immediate' in the Act's terms requiring 'to be put into immediate operation adequate means of reversing the air current.' His argument posed more questions than it answered and did not explain away the long delay in meeting the obligations of the Act.

In answering the charge concerning the use of safety lamps not of an approved type Kenshole pointed out that the objection was not to the design of the lamp but to the type of glass fitted to the lamps used at the colliery. Shaw gave evidence of having ordered 12 dozen glasses from one maker and 60 dozen from another. When he gave the orders he thought he would be supplied with approved glasses but the last lot received on 13th August 1913 did not have the approved mark on them. He also told the court that, following the issue of a circular by the Home Office on 25th August 1913 about the use of approved glass, there had been great difficulty in obtaining approved glasses from manufacturers. Dr. Atkinson agreed this had been the case.

The two charges relating to the measurement of the quantity of air in the main air current and at every split were considered together. In his evidence J. Dyer Lewis, one of the mines' inspectors, recalled Shaw's admission at the inquiry, in reply to questions from William Brace and Tom Richards, that air measurements had not been taken at the places stipulated in the Act. Shaw's contention, it will be remembered, was that there could be no loss of air between the points at which he had taken the measurements and those where the Act required them to be taken.

For his part Kenshole argued that technically there had been no violation of the legal requirements inasmuch as measurements had been taken under the old requirements only three weeks before the explosion. The new provision requiring a monthly reading came into force on 16th September 1913; thus, he argued, there was no obligation to have taken measurements until one month later on 16th October — two days after the explosion.

At this juncture the magistrates adjourned the hearing until 4th July 1914 leaving the evidence on the charges relating to the book entries for air current measurements and the control of coal dust to be heard then.

The first charges heard at the resumed hearing in July were the two relating to Shaw's failure to clear and failing to cause to be cleared coal dust from floor, roof and sides of roads. At the suggestion of Ivor Bowen, for the prosecution, the Clerk to the Court, R. Y. Evans, agreed the two charges should be taken as one. Bowen then went on to point out that the requirement to clear coal dust as far as reasonably practicable had not the slightest concern with cost or profit; the practicability was directed at eliminating danger.

Among the witnesses Bowen called were a number of Inspectors of Mines, from both Wales and England. Dr W. N. Atkinson of the South Wales Division gave evidence how, at the inquiry, Shaw admitted that nothing had been done at Senghenydd for some time to clear coal dust from the roof and sides of roads. He admitted, when cross-examined by Charles Kenshole, that removal of coal dust by blowing with compressed air carried the dust into the coal faces with attendant increase in danger from shot firing. He would not advise the use of this method of clearance if he was in charge of the mine.

Hugh Johnson, Inspector of Mines from the Midland Division in England, gave evidence of his experience of brushing coal dust from roof and sides with dry brushes. He said this method had proved effective in preventing coal dust accumulating and had cleared workings of a large proportion of coal dust. Charles Robinson, another inspector for an English Division, confirmed the practicability of the brushing process; the only danger was if shot firing was carried out at the same time as brushing was taking place — but this was avoidable.

Thomas Henry Mottram, an inspector from the Yorkshire and North Midlands Division explained how effective the application of stone dust to roofs and sides had been in some collieries.

Kenshole in defence dismissed the practice of stone dusting as irrelevant to the charge which was concerned only with the clearance of coal dust. He went on to express his astonishment at any suggestion that owners and management were bound to clear coal dust from roofs and sides whatever the effect may be; he felt this was certainly not a proper interpretation of the Act's intention on this matter.

Among the witnesses he called were David Hannah, mining engineer of Ferndale, Thomas Griffiths, managing director of Messrs Insoles Ltd, and Edward Shaw.

Hannah gave evidence of the danger involved in removing coal dust by compressed air and its consequent dispersal elsewhere, whilst Griffiths said experiments had shown the clearing of coal dust resulted in a greater quantity of it finding its way into and being deposited in the coal faces.

Shaw admitted the danger of fine coal dust but told the court everything conceivable had been tried, and no expense spared to clear it in his mine. Arching the roads had been tried but the 'squeeze' crushed the arches and this was discontinued. Dusting was tried for about six months but found impracticable. Brushing, in his opinion, resulted in at least ten per cent of the displaced dust accumulating in the coal faces.

The final three summonses — all taken together — concerned the lack of book entries in respect of air measurements. Here again Kenshole deployed his previous argument that there was no obligation under the new provisions to record these measurements until 16th October 1913. For the company he argued they had no case to answer against the charge of failing to provide a book to record these measurements; they were absolved inasmuch as Shaw had been provided with funds for thorough management of the mine.

The magistrates adjourned the hearing to 18th July 1914 when their decision on all charges would be given.

On the due date these decisions were announced. They left miners, their union and the mines inspectorate appalled, amazed and disgusted.

In pronouncing judgement the chairman of the bench commented on individual charges or a number of similar charges taken together and gave decisions accordingly.

They found Shaw guilty of failing to appoint the surface lamp man in writing in that he had relied on the appointment in 1905 when the colliery was taken over by the company. The plea of guilty to the failure to appoint the underground lamp locker resulted in the bench returning the same verdict on each of these appointment charges; on each Shaw was fined £2 with costs of £5 5s (£5.25) or fourteen days imprisonment in the second division.

Schielbach's evidence concerning the appointment of the colliery electrician was accepted and this charge was dismissed.

Shaw was found guilty on all three charges affecting the provision of a book and recording therein the daily readings of the thermometer, barometer and hygrometer. On the combined charges he was fined £5 with costs of £5 5s (£5.25p) or fourteen days imprisonment in the second division. The charge against the colliery company of failing to provide a book for these readings was dismissed.

The failure to provide means of immediately reversing the air current was considered by the mines' inspectorate to be of extreme gravity, particularly in view of the extension granted to management to ensure its completion. This gravity was not reflected in the judgement delivered by the chairman when he said 'it has been proved to our satisfaction that on

14th October 1913 this work had not been carried out or that, at all events, it was not completed. There was a non-compliance with the Act and we fine the defendant £10 with costs of £5 5s (£5.25p) or one month imprisonment in the second division.' They dismissed the similar charge against the company.

The other extremely serious charges were those affecting the clearance of coal dust from floor, roof and sides of roads. The decision of the bench makes one wonder whether they fully appreciated the danger presented by fine coal dust in the workings, whether they were aware of the findings of the inquiry into the 1901 explosion and Galloway's recommendations subsequent to it, and whether they recognised the full import of the requirements of the 1911 Act. They should have done so as justices in a mining area — but they did not. Both charges against Shaw were dismissed — and justified by the chairman in these terms:-

> We are satisfied that the defendant had endeavoured by means of brushing, compressed air blowing, by using stone dust and by watering to clear the roof and the sides of the roads from coal dust. The brushing and compressed air methods were abandoned by default some four to six months before 14th October 1913 because they were not found to be satisfactory. The comparable efficiency of the methods of brushing and air blowing was contradicted by specialist evidence . . . With the conflicting evidence which has been given before us we are placed in a position of great difficulty in arriving at our decision — but having given the question our serious and careful consideration we have come to the conclusion that the manager had done all that was reasonably practicable under the circumstances to prevent the accumulation of coal dust and we, therefore, dismiss the informations.'

And yet this was the same bench of justices which went on to fine Shaw on the two charges affecting his failure to report the conditions relating to coal dust in the roads and on the steps taken to mitigate this danger. On these two charges taken together Shaw was fined £5 with £5 5s costs or fourteen days in the second division.

All the remaining charges against Shaw — five concerning the measurement and recording of air currents and one relating to unapproved safety lamps — and the two against the company — one each for air currents measurements and safety lamps — were dismissed.

The dismissal of the charges against the colliery company was justified by the chairman of the bench in these words:- 'The company had taken all the necessary steps to enforce the Act and the rules. They had appointed a competent certificated manager, who was also the agent, and he had the sole contract, management and direction of the colliery; that the directors of the company took no part, nor did they interfere in the management; that the company made all the financial and other provisions necessary to enable the manager to carry out his duties; that the offences alleged in these proceedings were committed without their knowledge, consent or connivance of the company. We therefore dismiss the informations against the company.'

Of the seventeen charges against Edward Shaw nine had been dismissed and the eight remaining convictions resulted in fines amounting to £24.

The public reaction to this travesty of justice was widespread and immediate. One local paper described how the death of 440 men resulted in fines amounting to £24 — and scathingly headlined its report of the court decisions 'Miners' Lives at 1s 1¼d each' (5½p).

Professor H. S. Jevons in his book *The British Coal Trade* pointed out the paucity of the fines imposed compared with the seriousness of the failure to reverse the air current which possibly would have prevented the loss of 100 lives. Also the failure to deal with the coal dust had aggravated the severity and extent of the explosion.

The Miners' Federation were quick to react to the outcome of the court proceedings. The Executive Committee of the Miners' Federation of Great Britain immediately condemned the court's decision and sought a meeting with the Home Secretary to discuss the findings.

The result was that the Inspector of Mines for the South Wales Division, with the approval of the Home Secretary, filed appeals to the Court of Appeal in two of the dismissed charges. One was in respect of the colliery company's failure to provide for the immediate reversal of the air current and the other covered Edward Shaw's failure to remove coal dust from the roof and sides of roads. The appeal against Shaw's coal dust charge was dismissed in the autumn of 1914 whilst the appeal against the dismissal of the charge against the owners was sent back to the local magistrates by the Appeal Court for further information. In 1915 the Court of the King's Bench allowed this appeal and sent the case back to the magistrates to convict.

The important aspect of this direction was that the Court of Appeal had decided that the failure to provide the means to reverse the air current

The party of inquest jurymen, with mine officials, which examined the colliery workings during the inquest hearing *(permission of the National Museum of Wales)*

meant that the mine was not managed in conformity with the Act and that the owners, agent and manager were consequently guilty of an offence against the 1911 Coal Mines Act. This meant the Court of Appeal then had to decide whether the escape provision contained in Section 102 of the Act obtained to the owner. These clauses made an owner not liable to penalty if he was able to prove 'to the satisfaction of the court . . . (1) that he was not in the habit of taking and did not . . . take any part in the management of the mine and . . . (2) that the offence was committed without his knowledge, consent or connivance.' The Court decided the owners had failed to satisfy the requirements of the Act on both these points.

This single charge was heard again by the same magistrates (W. W. Ware and G. E. Forestier-Walker) on 22nd February 1916. They found the charge proven and fined the colliery company £10 with £5 5s costs.

This decision, whilst it was derisory in cash terms, at least restored the standing of the 1911 Act, with all its sensible and stringent safety requirements, and effectively scotched any attempts by other mine owners to treat it lightly or as just one more set of rules to be ignored.

Lord Merthyr of Senghenydd was destined to have no knowledge of the outcome of these appeals. Some six weeks after the local magistrates had passed judgement on the original charges, Lord Merthyr joined his ancestors. He died on 29th August 1914.

Whatever else is written or said about these legal proceedings the local magistrates, by their light sentences, obviously failed to see the point made by Redmayne in §134 of his report. There he wrote:-

> Some of these breaches . . . may appear trivial, but taken in the aggregate they point to a disquieting laxity in the management of the mine.

In missing this crucial point the bench of magistrates cannot avoid the criticism that they failed to appreciate the enormity of the disaster resulting from failure to comply with legal provisions.

The last word surely lies with a Senghenydd miner who was fortunate to come out of the Universal Colliery on 14th October 1913. He never returned to work underground. In describing his experiences William Hyatt said, "My father always said there was more fuss if a horse was killed underground than if a man was killed. Men came cheap — they had to buy horses."

Chapter 11

Epilogue

TO ALL INTENTS and purposes that was the end of the Senghenydd story — but no story really ends when the last sentence has been written. Life still had to go on in the Aber Valley.

For those who lost husbands, fathers and sons in the explosion the paralysing misery of their immediate loss was to be followed by a lifelong deprivation of the presence and earning capacity of their dead menfolk. Each affected family was to have its own story of trauma and hardship and the full account of the Senghenydd explosion will forever be incomplete while each of those stories remains untold. So one can only generalise on the overall effect and instance how some individuals recognised the impact on the valley's villages of the death of so many wage earners.

Extracts from writings by two authors capture the effect on communities of a large death roll like that at the Universal Colliery and for this reason they deserve to be quoted.

In her book *South Riding* Winifred Holtby describes how schoolmistress Sarah Burton cogitates on the death of men in World War 1 in these terms:-

> With increasing awareness every year she realised what it had meant of horror, desperation, anxiety and loss to her generation. She knew that the dead are most needed, not when they are mourned, but in a world robbed of their stabilising presence.

The other excerpt is from *Great Pit Disasters – Great Britain – 1700 to the Present Day* by Helen and Baron Duckham and runs:-

> A colliery disaster strikes and withers a whole community. The toll of a shipwreck or the carnage of a rail or air disaster is more promiscuous, picking on men and women from many areas and many walks of life. Even an earthquake or a flood,

> infinitely more terrible though their effects may be, lack one peculiarity. They may obliterate a town or even a region, but they do not discriminate according to sex. A mining accident of large proportions, on the other hand, sweeps away the menfolk of a whole settlement, leaving widows and children, sisters and sweethearts alone to face an uncertain future. Only old-fashioned conventional war can be comparable in its perverse depredation, as when a local regiment is decimated in action. The colliery disaster, too, was historically almost unique in hitting that strata of society least able to provide for the sudden death of its breadwinner and for long least powerful politically. Perhaps if the middle classes had been those on whom such catastrophes were so regularly visited in the nineteenth century, inspection and adequate safety regulations would have become law more quickly than in fact they did.

The 'sudden death of its breadwinner' had robbed the families of the Aber Valley of their 'stabilising presence' and their earnings. Now their womenfolk, children and relatives were dependent on the relief funds initiated by the Miners' Federation and lord mayors, including those of London and Cardiff. Among many other funds set up were those in Newport, Swansea, Merthyr Tydfil, Barry, Neath, Aberdare, Caerphilly, Margam, Ebbw Vale and Abercarn.

Eventually all these were amalgamated and became one relief fund administered by a committee representing all the interested parties both communal and mining. The residue of the fund initiated by the South Wales Miners' Federation, for example, stood at over £13,800 when it was handed over in July 1914 — but more than £126,000 had been collected by all the various funds since their inception. This amount had to provide for over 800 dependants of those killed — and for many of them the provision had to be for life.

The general level of weekly payments allowed 10 shillings (50p) for a widow or adult dependant with 5 shillings (25p) for a child. With at least 205 widows, 542 children and 62 dependent fathers and mothers this implied annual payments amounting to over £10,000. It speaks well for the astuteness and perspicacity of the Fund's committee that by 1951 £195,353 had been disbursed. This meant that nearly £70,000 had been added to the fund by judicious investment.

Charity of this sort was felt by the strongly independent communities of the mining valleys of South Wales to be both a slur and an indignity and its acceptance did not lie lightly on their stomachs. But widows with young mouths to feed and no-one to provide for them had no other option. The same applied to aged parents and other dependants. Nevertheless the evidence in the records of the Fund committee is that claims were considered humanely, sympathetically and, within the constraints of husbanding limited resources, even generously.

In many ways the administration of the fund was enlightened and in advance of its time. The minutes record that grants were made for children in ill health, children continuing at school, to guardians of orphans, to cover payment of apprenticeship premiums, to provide uniforms for girls becoming nurses etc. and for teeth, spectacles and special needs of both children and adults. There were cases of widows who remarried and ceased to be recipients under the Fund; on the death of the second husband (dependent on circumstances), some were reinstated as beneficiaries.

But money was no substitute for menfolk.

For some women their loss was more than one could possibly shoulder. And yet who was to say which was the worst hit of all the stricken women in the valley?

Mrs Ross of 22 Coronation Terrace lost her husband, two sons, a brother and a young man who lodged with them — with five dead was hers the greatest loss?

Or was it worse for Mrs Jenkins whose son, Thomas Jenkins of 12 Kingsley Place, and her grandson were both killed? In 1894 two of her sons had been killed in the explosion at the Albion Colliery at Cilfynydd. In the 1901 Senghenydd explosion a son and a son-in-law had been killed. Was her misery the most painful?

Or did this doubtful honour fall to Mrs Baker of 18 Alexandra Terrace, Senghenydd, whose husband and 14 year old son had both been killed leaving her with a newly born babe and ten other children?

Could it have been Mary Jane Lewis, a 28 year old teacher in the Senghenydd school? She was due to marry David John Davies of Commercial Street who died in the Pretoria District. She never did so; when she died in 1977 she was 93 years old and still unmarried.

It was none of these; it was all of them.

There was no comparative worst hit case — to each family their own was the worst.

The whole community had been blighted by an explosive spark below ground that had shuddered and shaken the foundations of every aspect of the valley's life. Chapels and churches found they had lost most of their deacons, sidesmen and officials. The valley's male voice choir had lost a goodly number of its members with little likelihood of replacements until young boys grew to take their place. And the miners who had escaped the effects of the explosion had also lost. They had lost many of their friends — the friends with whom they had enjoyed a drink, a joke, a chat, a game of cards and a leisurely stroll.

Theo. Lewis of Plas Cwm Parc, Senghenydd was one of those who was fortunate to come out of the mine alive, but it is indelibly scarred into his memory that he lost eight friends in the disaster. When he can be prevailed upon to recount his own story of that October morning he is near to tears — even now, nearly seventy years later — when he recalls how he was one of ten lads who were friends and went everywhere together in the evenings and at weekends. All ten of them worked in the Senghenydd mine — only two survived the explosion. Theo. Lewis himself was one.

After the explosion some of the miners left the colliery and found safer work at other mines or as coal trimmers loading 'colliers' in the docks at Cardiff. Others, like William Hyatt who became a pawnbroker's assistant, took any employment available which had no association with coal mining. But for everyone who left there were many ready to take their place. The level of wages paid in the coal mines were still an attraction of gold rush proportions to the agricultural workers of Mid Wales, Gloucestershire and Somerset. The Universal Colliery had no difficulty in replacing its lost workforce.

But the outbreak of war with Germany in August 1914 attracted many of the valley's younger men who were seduced into serving their country by the recruiting sergeant's call. Young William Hyatt was one of sixty who left the valley for the Forces in one day in 1914. Of the many who followed them the names of sixty-two are recorded on the war memorial at Senghenydd and eighty-two on that at Abertridwr. In the seventeen years from 1901 the valley thus suffered the sudden death of over 600 of its menfolk.

This continual drain of male blood from the valley was forcibly spotlighted in the comment of Bryn Edwards, ironmonger at Senghenydd for many years and a former member of the village rugby team. In discussing the effect of the explosion and the 1914–18 war on the village he said, "When I was playing rugby for Senghenydd in 1916 thirteen of the team were under the age of 16 — there were so few older players."

And yet the moral strength of this community enabled it to overcome these massive trials and the further tribulations of the mining and industrial disputes of 1921 and 1926. These traumatic years were followed by the crushing blow of the closure of the Universal Colliery in 1928. Although the Powell Duffryn Company took over the colliery in 1931, to use its workings to augment the ventilation of the Windsor Colliery at Abertridwr, it was never worked again as a productive coal mine. The financial depression of the late 1920s and the 1930s meant the valley saw more than its share of unemployment and poverty, with its consequent migration of the young to other areas where there were better chances of work.

Then the government's policy of diversifying industry, in hitherto one industry areas, by building industrial estates like the one at Treforest, near Caerphilly, began to alleviate unemployment and staunch this flow of young blood from the area. Even so, it took another war to bring some semblance of prosperity to the valley. Once more coal production assumed increased importance to provide the power to fight the war against Hitler, while women were required to provide replacements for the men called to the Forces. When the war ended in 1945 the role of women and wives in the home had altered radically. In the mining valleys of South Wales the pattern of women going out to work was established by the war and, with it, the long haul away from dependence on one industry — with its attendant menace of unemployment — had begun. It also signalled a move towards a more prosperous future for Senghenydd and Abertridwr. This is now reflected in new house-building, private ownership of houses and improvement and decorative face-lifting of older properties in the valley. The indications are that the valley and its people have overcome the disasters which emanated from its colliery.

And what of the colliery and its manager?

It would be natural to expect that the name of Edward Shaw engenders little respect in Senghenydd. His involvement in two major disasters, his conviction on the charges of negligence and Redmayne's report of laxity in management would justify this assumption. But such is not the case — and it is only fair to Shaw and his family to record this.

Those old enough to know him or know about him always refer to him as Teddy Shaw — a diminutive which reflects the respect, and even affection, of the community for the man. Men who survived the explosion recall him as 'a good man,' 'a God-fearing man' and 'a manager who looked after his workmen' — accolades indeed from usually laconic miners. Theo. Lewis goes even further and recalls him as 'the bravest man I ever knew,' this reflects the acknowledgement accorded Shaw by Thomas Richards and Robert Redmayne at the public inquiry into the 1913 explosion.

And the colliery? After its final closure it gradually became derelict, an eyesore and a danger. In 1963 it was decided to demolish the mouldering

The derelict colliery in the 1950s
(permission of the County of Mid Glamorgan Libraries — Pontypridd Branch)

The York Pit in process of demolition in 1963

pit-head buildings and the winding gear over the two pits. By an ironic and macabre touch the colliery known for its underground explosions was ultimately demolished above ground by the same means.

In March 1963 the No 100 Squadron of the Royal Monmouthshire Royal Engineers (Militia) laid explosive charges which demolished the old engine house and some of the derelict surface buildings. The winding gear above the Lancaster pit was dismantled followed by that of the York pit. Finally the site was levelled and a saw mill was built where the colliery once stood. In the summer of 1979 the two shafts were filled with rocks and rubble and capped with concrete to seal them off.

So time seems to have obliterated the surface scars of the Universal Colliery and nearly healed the wounds it inflicted. The miners who survived the events of that October morning grow fewer each year, as do those who were affected by the death roll. As their numbers become fewer so the number increases to whom the tragedy of Senghenydd means little or nothing. There is no easily obtainable record of those who died; there is no memorial to them or those who suffered their loss.

The nearest approach to such a memorial at present is a cluster of graves in the churchyard of St Ilan's Church on the mountainside at Eglwysilan above Abertridwr. There, within an area of 15 yards radius, lying shoulder to shoulder and head to toe are the graves of some of the men who died in the explosions in the Senghenydd colliery in 1901 and 1913. In eight graves lie ten men who died in the earlier explosion — George Warren, Thomas Coombes, Jacob Lewis, George Lower, Phillip Lower, John Walters, David Vaughan, John Thomas, William Rowland and William David Rowland.

Behind the west of these lies a single grave of white marble, now moss and lichen covered, which stands as a reminder that there were other mining disasters affecting other valley communities — and adding to the tally of blood spilled by the winning of coal. It is the grave of Elias Roberts of Llanarman Row, Bwlchgwyn and his epitaph records, in Welsh, how he died on the 11th July 1905 in the Wattstown explosion. This was an explosion at the National Colliery at Wattstown, in the Rhondda Fach valley on 11th July 1905; in it 119 men died.

Around this grave lie those of four men who died later in 'the Senghenydd explosion' of 1913. Their graves enclose the remains of William Hyatt senior and Brynley Hyatt, David Thomas Richards and David Hughes.

One could see in these graves some sort of memorial to the suffering and sorrow coal brought to South Wales in general and this small community in particular — or without knowing what happened at Senghenydd in 1901 and 1913, see them as just more graves in another churchyard.

It is reported that a memorial to the men who died in 'the Senghenydd explosion' is to be erected near the sealed shafts of the Universal Colliery. It is unlikely to record any of the suffering caused to this valley community. This account was written to fill — if only partially — that gap.

"Boast not thyself of to-morrow; for thou knowest not what a day may bring forth."

In Loving Memory

OF THE

434 COLLIERS,

— WHO —

Lost their Lives in the terrible colliery explosion

— AT —

The Universal Pits, at Senghenydd,
On October 14th, 1913.

Early on Friday morning, May 24th, 1901, 81 poor Miners lost their lives in the same pits.

The Memorial Card reproduced here was provided by Mrs Irene Coombes

APPENDIX I

Death Roll of the Explosion on 24th May 1901

Name	*Age*	*Address*
1. George Warren	61	44 Stanley Street, Senghenydd
2. John Jones	32	15 Kingsley Place, Senghenydd
3. Thomas Coombes	29	26 High Street, Senghenydd
4. George Griffiths	59	23 Parc Terrace, Senghenydd
5. John Davies	25	137 Commercial St, Senghenydd
6. David Morgan	—	4 Bartlett Street, Caerphilly
7. Lewis C. Hurley	—	22 Grove Terrace, Senghenydd
8. William T. Evans	33	5 The Huts, Senghenydd
9. Bob Rowlands	—	Commercial Street, Senghenydd
10. Llewellyn Llewellyn	—	10 Parc Terrace, Senghenydd
11. Albert Edward Lee	28	14 Station Terrace, Senghenydd
12. John Evans	54	High Street, Senghenydd
13. David Jones	26	103 Commercial St, Senghenydd
14. David Jenkins	29	14 Grove Terrace, Senghenydd
15. George Griffiths	25	135 Commercial St, Senghenydd
16. John Phelps	26	7 The Huts, Senghenydd
17. Thomas Fullerlove	—	42 Stanley Street, Senghenydd
18. Joseph Fullerlove	17	42 Stanley Street, Senghenydd
19. William J. Lewis	—	33 Thomas Street, Abertridwr
20. William Morgan	20	4 Bartlett Street, Caerphilly
21. John Harvey	19	Stanley Street, Senghenydd
22. Philip Lower	18	Yorkshire Hall, Abertridwr
23. William John	21	9 Station Terrace, Senghenydd
24. James James	29	47 Caerphilly Road, Senghenydd
25. James Edwards	30	17 Ilan Road, Abertridwr
26. Henry Layman	36	30 Parc Terrace, Senghenydd
27. William Chas. Jones	30	57 Caerphilly Road, Senghenydd
28. Edward Bennett	39	31 Caerphilly Road, Senghenydd
29. William Trotman	32	18 Grove Terrace, Senghenydd

30. Jacob Lewis	—	*not quoted*
31. George Filer	—	35 High Street, Senghenydd
32. David Vaughan	—	7 High Street, Abertridwr
33. Rowland W. Rowland	—	4Caerphilly Road, Senghenydd
34. Thomas Fisher	—	24 High Street, Senghenydd
35. John Davies	36	35 Station Terrace, Senghenydd
36. Charles Henry Crocket	—	12 Ilan Road, Abertridwr
37. William Davies	—	Station Terrace, Senghenydd
38. David Bowles	31	14 The Huts, Senghenydd
39. Benjamin David Griffiths	33	91 Commercial St., Senghenydd
40. David Skym	17	17 Thomas Street, Abertridwr
41. Thomas Trefoil	57	1 Grove Terrace, Senghenydd
42. George Lower	26	Yorkshire Hall, Abertridwr
43. William David Rowland	24	49 Caerphilly Road, Senghenydd
44. David James	43	126 Commercial St., Senghenydd
45. Albert Lewis	19	12 The Huts, Senghenydd
46. George Whitfield	51	84 Caerphilly Road, Senghenydd
47. William Davies	36	29 Caerphilly Road, Senghenydd
48. Jonah Davies	59	14 Parc Terrace, Senghenydd
49. William Sheil	49	50 Stanley Street, Senghenydd
50. Evan John Jenkins	—	59 High Street, Senghenydd
51. William Anslow	—	High Street, Senghenydd
52. David Griffiths	52	Caerphilly Road, Senghenydd
53. Evan Williams	33	39 High Street, Senghenydd
54. William Thomas	51	51 High Street, Senghenydd
55. Robert Jones	36	137 Commercial St., Senghenydd
56. John Pugh	—	13 The Huts, Senghenydd
57. William Crook	42	56 Commercial St., Senghenydd
58. Thomas Williams	53	55 High Street, Senghenydd
59. Henry Jones	25	Bedwas
60. Thomas Morgan	35	16 Grove Terrace, Senghenydd
61. Rees Thomas	39	41 High Street, Abertridwr
62. Franz Muller	40	7 High Street, Abertridwr
63. Thomas Dobson	26	21 Caerphilly Road, Senghenydd
64. John Thomas	31	56 Stanley Street, Senghenydd
65. John Walters	—	24 Caerphilly Road, Senghenydd
66. Albert Blackmore	33	146 Commercial St., Senghenydd
67. William Williams	49	46 High Street, Abertridwr
68. Andrew Diegan	22	17 High Street, Senghenydd
69. John Thomas	34	3 Grove Terrace, Senghenydd

70. Gwilym Morgan	32	25 High Street, Abertridwr
71. William Parry	39	40 Station Terrace, Senghenydd
72. William Jenkin Jones	23	113 Commercial St., Senghenydd
73. John Thomas	43	45 Stanley Street, Senghenydd
74. Thomas Jones	35	High Street, Senghenydd
75. George Evans	—	The Twyn, Caerphilly
76. Thomas Jones	—	Station Terrace, Senghenydd
77. Ebenezer Davies	—	12 Grove Terrace, Senghenydd
78. Christopher Martin	—	High Street, Senghenydd
79. Gwilym Jones	—	High Street, Abertridwr
80. David Davies	—	12 Grove Terrace, Senghenydd
81. William Parker	—	High Street, Senghenydd

The list is compiled from the official Report to the Secretary of State for the Home Department (Cd. 947) and newspaper reports of the time. These sources did not, in many cases, provide details of age and full address of individuals; for this reason the list is comprehensive in respect of the names of the deceased only.

The last body — that of William Parker — was recovered on 24th February 1902

APPENDIX II

Death Roll of the Explosion on 14th October 1913

In compiling this list of the names of those killed in this explosion recourse has been made to three sources. These were:-

- the record of the Inquest proceedings;
- the report of the official Inquiry (Cd 7346);
- newspaper reports.

These sources confirm the death of 440 persons as a result of the explosion (i.e. 439 killed by the explosion itself and one rescuer killed the following day), but provide names and addresses of only 436 of the dead.

These are named in the following three lists:-

List A — The Inquest proceedings at Senghenydd

This list of 422 persons provides details of the bodies recovered from the mine by the time the inquest was reconvened at Senghenydd in January 1914. Although the dead are numbered from 1 to 420 in the list numbers 51 and 210 are duplicated as 51a and 210a — with 51a being William John, the rescuer who was killed by a fall. Also the list includes eight bodies recorded as unknown or unidentified — viz. numbers 16, 47, 53, 68, 98, 108, 315 and 419.

List B — The Official Report of the Inquiry (Cd 7346)

In an appendix to his report on the Official Inquiry R. A. S. Redmayne listed 429 persons whose bodies had been recovered. The difference between this total (429) and that of the inquest (422) is accounted for by the passage of time between the inquest and the preparation of Redmayne's report; in the meantime further bodies had been recovered. The list does not identify the dead by name and address — they are detailed by pit number and occupation.

Redmayne explains that, of the number recovered, 421 had been identified and the remaining eight had been buried unidentified — this latter figure accords with the inquest details. Among the 421 identified victims were seven who were brought out of the pit alive but who died subsequently at home or in hospital.

As part of the same appendix, but in a separate list, Redmayne set out the names, addresses, age and occupations of 19 other persons. This list included the eight victims who had been buried unidentified but who could not be distinguished from the eleven persons whose bodies were still buried beneath falls in the mine. These figures bring the total number of victims to 440 (viz. 421 identified, 8 unidentified — totalling 429 recovered — with 11 to be recovered).

List B sets out the names and addresses of these 19 persons.

List C — Compiled from Newspaper Reports

The three persons named in this list were those who died in hospital in Cardiff and whose death was reported as being investigated by the Coroner of that City.

Whilst there is no doubt at all that the total death roll was 440 these lists record the identity of only 436 of them — 414 from the inquest at Senghenydd, 19 from the inquiry report and three from the Cardiff inquest.

LIST A

Taken from the record of the Inquest Proceedings at Senghenydd

	Name	*Age*	*Address*
1.	John Williams	43	35 Cenydd Terrace, Senghenydd
2.	James Gwynn	44	3 De Barry Street, Rhydyfelin
3.	Edward Griffiths	18	3 De Barry Street, Rhydyfelin
4.	Griffith Roberts	20	40 Stanley Street, Senghenydd
5.	Charles Francis Anderson	32	12 Woodland Terr., Senghenydd
6.	Thomas Jenkins	—	12 Kingsley Place, Senghenydd
7.	John Herring	60	7 Cenydd Terrace, Senghenydd
8.	John Dillon	36	30 Alexandra Terr, Senghenydd
9.	Richard Rees	30	45 Dolyfelyn Street, Senghenydd
10.	Edwin George Thorne	—	30 High Street, Abertridwr
11.	Thomas John Richards	16	112 Caerphilly Road, Senghenydd
12.	John Jones	50	183 Commercial St, Senghenydd
13.	Edward Richard Lewis	50	176 Commercial St, Senghenydd
14.	Dennis Carroll	—	20 Francis Street, Abertridwr
15.	William Dew	39	13 Railway Terr, Tongwynlais
16.	*Unknown* (about 40 years)		
17.	Charles Owen	30	5 Station Road, Senghenydd

18. Robert Rook	49	36 Gwilym Street, Rhydyfelin
19. David Henry Hill	16	21 Parc Terrace, Senghenydd
20. Ernest Morgan	—	Ty Melyn House, Caerphilly
21. George Robert Hallett	14	36 Gwilym Street, Rhydyfelin
22. William Morgan jnr	20	Ty Melyn House, Caerphilly
23. William Morgan snr	46	Ty Melyn House, Caerphilly
24. David John Davies	34	17 The Huts, Senghenydd
25. Francis Lewis Morgan	35	16 White Street, Caerphilly
26. Thomas Henry Rees	21	29 Cenydd Terrace, Senghenydd
27. Edmund Jones	41	18 Station Road, Senghenydd
28. James Thomas	39	14 Brynhyfryd Terr, Senghenydd
29. Albert Edgar Dean	33	240 Nantgarw Road, Caerphilly
30. John Lot Peters	27	48 Bartlett Street, Caerphilly
31. John Frederick Carnell	47	25 Stanley Street, Senghenydd
32. Thomas Meredith	43	13 Grove Terrace, Senghenydd
33. William Griffith Hughes	22	60 High Street, Senghenydd
34. Taliesin Roberts	—	50 High Street, Abertridwr
35. John Rowlands	39	77 Mill Road, Caerphilly
36. George Davies	19	21 Station Terrace, Senghenydd
37. Samuel Booth	—	43 Edward Terrace, Abertridwr
38. Emrys Hughes Williams	20	64 High Street, Senghenydd
39. John Robinson	33	38 Graig Terrace, Senghenydd
40. William Ewart Uphill	15	1 Station Road, Senghenydd
41. Edward Gilbert	55	23 Coronation Terr, Senghenydd
42. William Francis Davies	27	46 Commercial St, Senghenydd
43. William John Rees	43	132 Commercial St, Senghenydd
44. Oliver Rees	19	61 Stanley Street, Senghenydd
45. John Hughes	—	21 Bridgefield Street, Abertridwr
46. David Jones	—	50 King Street, Abertridwr
47. *Unknown* (about 50)		
48. Charles Peters	22	12 North Luton Place, Adamsdown, Cardiff
49. William Hillborne	36	46 High Street, Senghenydd
50. John Mogridge	29	69 High Street, Senghenydd
51. William Chas. Thomas	21	21 Cenydd Terrace, Senghenydd
51a. William John	—	93 Thomas Street, Abertridwr
52. Edward Matthews	61	9 Station Terrace, Penyrheol
53. *Unknown* (about 40)		
54. David Evans	51	31 Parc Terrace, Senghenydd
55. John Howlett	39	48 High Street, Senghenydd

56. Humphrey Jones	43	134 Caerphilly Road, Senghenydd
57. Rowland Lewis	55	11 Caerphilly Road, Senghenydd
58. Peter Ronald Ross	20	5 Coronation Terr, Senghenydd
59. Evan Hopkin James	42	24 Grove Terrace, Senghenydd
60. George Pingree	25	30 Coburn Street, Cardiff
61. Sidney Alfred Lasbury	26	15 Graig Terrace, Senghenydd
62. James Maher	37	14 Commercial St, Senghenydd
63. Timothy Carroll	35	20 Francis Street, Abertridwr
64. Henry John Brooks	25	159 Commercial St, Senghenydd
65. William Frank Waddon	22	28 Graig Terrace, Senghenydd
66. Frederick Alderman	45	159 Commercial St, Senghenydd
67. Mathew Henry Dorey	21	1 Windsor Place, Senghenydd
68. *Unknown* (5ft 8in long)		
69. William Baish	50	24 Cenydd Terrace, Senghenydd
70. Evan Weston	40	21 Grove Terrace, Senghenydd
71. William Williams	24	43 Stanley Street, Senghenydd
72. William Thomas Roberts	26	3 Station Terrace, Senghenydd
73. William Abel Jones	21	167 Commercial St, Senghenydd
74. Howell Thomas	38	5 Cwm Eldeg Cottages, Nr Cilfynydd
75. William Bishop	37	5 Cenydd Terrace, Senghenydd
76. Evan David Evans	22	31 Parc Terrace, Senghenydd
77. Thomas Davies Adams	19	3 Phillips Terrace, Senghenydd
78. Edward Lewis	23	10 Church Street, Abertridwr
79. James Etchells	34	92 Bedwas Road, Caerphilly
80. Glyndwr Williams	14	4 Woodland Terrace, Senghenydd
81. King Samuel Humphries	46	19 High Street, Senghenydd
82. James Lower	18	25 Coronation Terr, Senghenydd
83. William Hadley Pain	34	63 Coburn Street, Cardiff
84. John Philip Humphries	23	72 Commercial St, Senghenydd
85. Hugh Thomas	30	8 Stanley Street, Senghenydd
86. David Thos. Richards	37	2 Gelli Villas, Senghenydd
87. Rees Thomas	42	9 Caerphilly Road, Senghenydd
88. Joseph Thos. Lewis	31	31 High Street, Senghenydd
89. William Henry Hemmings	25	75 High Street, Senghenydd
90. Thomas Phillips	28	8 Stanley Street, Senghenydd
91. William Dodge	21	71 Nantgarw Road, Caerphilly
92. William Prosser	28	52 High Street, Senghenydd
93. William Bennett	33	10 James Street, Llanbradach
94. James David Edwards	33	43 Commercial St, Senghenydd

95.	Thomas Lewis	62	95 Commercial St, Senghenydd
96.	James Moran	24	22a High Street, Senghenydd
97.	Edward Morgan Lewis	51	188 Commercial St, Senghenydd
98.	*Unknown*		
99.	David Williams	53	19 Parc Terrace, Senghenydd
100.	Henry Hall	35	100 Commercial St, Senghenydd
101.	Albert John Griffiths	21	1 Wesleyan Chapel, Senghenydd
102.	Frank Ferris	39	78 High Street, Abertridwr
103.	Richard Morris Fern	19	44 Lower Francis St, Abertridwr
104.	David Jones	43	1 Woodland Terrace, Senghenydd
105.	Francis Humphries	33	17 High Street, Senghenydd
106.	Thomas Cronin	26	92 Bedwas Road, Caerphilly
107.	John Henry Witherall	24	55 De Winton Terr, Llanbradach
108.	*Unknown* (about 5ft 6in long)		
109.	Charles Parry	47	9 Parc Terrace, Senghenydd
110.	Thomas David Jones	19	138 Caerphilly Road, Senghenydd
111.	Richard Evans	25	71 High Street, Senghenydd
112.	Thomas Hearne	42	3 Graig Terrace, Senghenydd
113.	Richard Jones	43	38 Station Terrace, Senghenydd
114.	Rodney Austin Manning	40	147 Thomas Street, Abertridwr
115.	Francis Pitt Cotterell	21	49 Commercial St, Senghenydd
116.	George Herritts	22	169 Commercial St, Senghenydd
117.	Herbert James Delbridge	22	31 Parc Terrace, Senghenydd
118.	Robert John Evans	19	67 High Street, Senghenydd
119.	John Robert Davies	22	145 Commercial St, Senghenydd
120.	William Samuel Jones	27	2 Energlyn Crescent, Penyrheol
121.	Christopher Jones	25	1 Parc Cottages, Senghenydd
122.	Cadwaladr Wm. Morris	23	2 Brynhyfryd Terr, Senghenydd
123.	John Morris	31	18 Brynhyfryd Terr, Senghenydd
124.	Arthur Morgan Richards	24	112 Caerphilly Road, Senghenydd
125.	William Jones	24	2 Brynhyfryd Terr, Senghenydd
126.	David John James	34	16 Grove Terrace, Senghenydd
127.	Morgan Jones	31	8 The Huts, Senghenydd
128.	George William Coombes	22	48 Caerphilly Road, Senghenydd
129.	George Ford	17	32 High Street, Senghenydd
130.	George Bastyn	26	3 Cross Street, Senghenydd
131.	Frederick John Ford	35	13 Bridgefield Street, Abertridwr
132.	Joseph Arthur Lock	20	11 Woodland Terr, Senghenydd
133.	Charles Gordon Lewis	21	5 Nydfa Road, Pengam
134.	Morgan Roberts	27	16 Graig Terrace, Senghenydd

135. Frederick Williams	43	5 White Street, Caerphilly
136. Frank Bormeth	19	13 Energlyn Terrace, Penyrheol
137. Thomas James Morris	19	*Not stated*
138. Edwin Morris	23	43 High Street, Abertridwr
139. Walter Edwards	20	11 High Street, Senghenydd
140. Harry Boswell	49	50 High Street, Senghenydd
141. William Hugh Williams	39	31 Coronation Terr, Senghenydd
142. Thomas Evans	41	52 Commercial St, Senghenydd
143. Thomas Fern	20	44 Lower Francis St, Abertridwr
144. Arthur Henry Williams	19	25 Cenydd Terrace, Senghenydd
145. David John Jones	33	19 Station Terrace, Senghenydd
146. David John Lewis	24	11 Bridgefield Street, Abertridwr
147. Charles Emery	61	7 Thomas Street, Abertridwr
148. Thomas Propert Mendus	32	1 Upper Francis St, Abertridwr
149. Thos. John Joseph Collier	45	19 Sophia Street, Cardiff
150. Thomas Jones	36	40 King Street, Abertridwr
151. Charles James Jones	51	1 Woodland Terrace, Senghenydd
152. Evan Price Jones	32	26 Kingsley Place, Senghenydd
153. Richard John Edwards	20	44 Commercial St, Senghenydd
154. Idrisyn Humphries	31	147 Commercial St, Senghenydd
155. Evan Edwards	50	44 Commercial St, Senghenydd
156. John Thomas	31	34 High Street, Senghenydd
157. Ernest Edwards	25	16 Woodland Terr, Senghenydd
158. Charles Chard	30	25 St Cenydd Terr, Penyrheol
159. David James Rees	28	35 Stanley Street, Senghenydd
160. William Henly	43	38 Station Terrace, Senghenydd
161. Walter Berry	27	19 Ilan Road, Abertridwr
162. Thomas Saunders	21	28 Upper Francis St, Abertridwr
163. Albert Edward Pegler	29	12 Phillips Terrace, Senghenydd
164. Meyrick Morris	30	6 School Street, Senghenydd
165. William Frank Thomas	28	32 High Street, Senghenydd
166. Daniel Lewis	51	142 Commercial St, Senghenydd
167. Samuel Augustus Hoare	37	13 Lower Brynyfryd Terrace, Senghenydd
168. Thomas Ivor Lewis	44	37 Caerphilly Road, Senghenydd
169. William Jones	36	32 Parc Terrace, Senghenydd
170. Henry Walsh	40	94 Thomas Street, Senghenydd
171. Albert Edward Pritchard	38	30 Commercial St, Senghenydd
172. Daniel John	26	68 High Street, Senghenydd
173. John White	33	7 Grove Terrace, Senghenydd

174.	David Francis Griffiths	28	125 Commercial St, Senghenydd
175.	Richard Matthews	37	12 Station Terrace, Senghenydd
176.	Richard Seager	26	20 Grove Terrace, Senghenydd
177.	William Morgan	35	14 Brynhyfryd Terr., Senghenydd
178.	John Richards	34	169 Commercial St, Senghenydd
179.	Charles Evans	38	40 Caerphilly Road, Senghenydd
180.	Thomas Thomas	28	101 Ilan Road, Abertridwr
181.	George Henry Downes	20	20 Caerphilly Road, Senghenydd
182.	Isaac James Taylor	25	37 Graig Terrace, Senghenydd
183.	Robert Bateman	18	18 High Street, Senghenydd
184.	William Henry White	24	101 Caerphilly Rd, Senghenydd
185.	William Thomas	24	33 High Street, Senghenydd
186.	William Eldridge	14	14 High Street, Senghenydd
187.	Thomas Deere	41	25 Stanley Street, Senghenydd
188.	Hugh Parry	28	110 Caerphilly Rd, Senghenydd
189.	Joseph Williams	26	2 Bryncoed Terrace, Abertridwr
190.	Samuel John Manfield	16	45 Planet St, Adamsdown, Cardiff
191.	Griffith Roberts	20	84 High Street, Senghenydd
192.	Jeffrey James Davies	28	31 Stanley Street, Senghenydd
193.	Richard Hunt	34	17 The Huts, Senghenydd
194.	Silas Lock	17	43 Stanley Street, Senghenydd
195.	Richard Stephen Rex	47	14 Phillips Terrace, Senghenydd
196.	Walter Grainger	22	63 Bartlett Street, Caerphilly
197.	Thomas Downes	19	20 Caerphilly Rd, Senghenydd
198.	George Henry Downes	43	20 Caerphilly Rd, Senghenydd
199.	Reginald Harrison	18	19 Cenydd Terrace, Senghenydd
200.	Albert Parish	29	3 Cross Street, Senghenydd
201.	George Thos. Harrison	45	19 Cenydd Terrace, Senghenydd
202.	Griffith Robert Lewis	21	84 High Street, Senghenydd
203.	Rowland Edward Lewis	19	84 High Street, Senghenydd
204.	Rowland Lewis	45	84 High Street, Senghenydd
205.	William Davies	43	42 Kingsley Place, Senghenydd
206.	Edwin John Small	21	25 Cenydd Terrace, Senghenydd
207.	Gwilym Morgan Rees	29	80 High Street, Senghenydd
208.	James Chas Henry Edwards	37	10 Alexandra Terr, Senghenydd
209.	Ruben Jones	14	19 Phillips Terrace, Senghenydd
210.	Thos. Henry Chas Cooke	15	220 Nantgarw Road, Caerphilly
210a.	Edward James	16	109 Thomas Street, Abertridwr
211.	William Joseph Hyatt	47	51 Caerphilly Road, Senghenydd

212. Joseph Hopkins	35	33 High Street, Senghenydd
213. Charles Moss	20	45 Commercial St, Senghenydd
214. William John Evans	22	104 High Street, Senghenydd
215. John Richard Kirkham	19	67 High Street, Senghenydd
216. John Kelly	22	4 Graig Terrace, Senghenydd
217. Charles Baker	14	18 Alexandra Terr, Senghenydd
218. Ezra Twining	30	20 Station Terrace, Senghenydd
219. Richard Owen Jones	18	134 Caerphilly Rd., Senghenydd
220. William Hughes	19	5 Station Terrace, Senghenydd
221. Frederick Walters	20	224 Nantgarw Road, Caerphilly
222. Enoch Rees Thomas	23	66 High Street, Senghenydd
223. James Colley	45	13 Henry Street, Bargoed
224. John Maddocks	42	8 Woodland Terr, Senghenydd
225. Thomas Maddocks	16	8 Woodland Terr, Senghenydd
226. Benjamin Jones	34	1 Station Terrace, Senghenydd
227. Rhys Jones Evans	48	189 Caerphilly Rd, Senghenydd
228. Stanford Heziciah Dando	27	57 Caerphilly Rd, Senghenydd
229. David Richard Evans	20	25 Caerphilly Rd, Senghenydd
230. Llewellyn Williams	21	17 Bryn Gelli Terr, Abertridwr
231. Robert Ross	31	22 Coronation Terr, Senghenydd
232. Chas Fred Hill	37	48 Pontygwindy Rd, Caerphilly
233. Benjamin Morgan	19	27 Grove Terrace, Senghenydd
234. John Thos. Bowen Jones	34	4 Phillips Terrace, Senghenydd
235. Edward Samuel Small	44	25 Cenydd Terrace, Senghenydd
236. Philip Lower	22	17 St Cenydd Terr, Penyrheol
237. Thomas Kestell	23	79 High Street, Senghenydd
238. Richard Davies Kestell	55	79 High Street, Senghenydd
239. John Jones	34	31 Cenydd Terrace, Senghenydd
240. Gilbert Whitcombe	37	1 Universal Huts, Senghenydd
241. Harry Jones	33	5 Graig Terrace, Senghenydd
242. Robert William Evans	38	26 Stanley Street, Senghenydd
243. James Bevan	32	4 Station Terrace, Senghenydd
244. Caleb Withers	56	52 Stanley Street, Senghenydd
245. Robert Eli Yardley	34	74 Nantgarw Road, Caerphilly
246. David Thomas	51	12 Alexandra Terr, Senghenydd
247. William Thos. Attewell	15	14 Pontygwindy Terr, Caerphilly
248. John Henry Scott	26	22 Graig Terrace, Senghenydd
249. John Carpenter	23	52 Dolyfelin Street, Caerphilly
250. Peter Carr	45	103 Commercial St, Senghenydd
251. Edwin Francis Bullock	30	14 Tonyfelin Road, Caerphilly

252. Benjamin Morris	38	43 Commercial St, Senghenydd
253. Benjamin Arthur Davies	25	46 Commercial St, Senghenydd
254. Alfred Charles Martin	23	54 Caerphilly Road, Senghenydd
255. James Davies	44	54 Caerphilly Road, Senghenydd
256. William Edward Beck	43	45 Springfield Terrace, Nelson
257. Noah Williams	50	52 Commercial St, Senghenydd
258. John Lewis Beynon	32	37 Bryn Gelli Terr, Abertridwr
259. Thomas James Cottrell	19	159 Commercial St, Senghenydd
260. Richard Henry Jones	16	Haulfryn, Brynhyfryd Terrace, Energlyn, Caerphilly
261. Patrick Williams	28	36 St Cenydd Terr, Penyrheol
262. Thomas Jones	20	10 St Cenydd Terr, Penyrheol
263. Arthur Vranch	19	30 Cenydd Terrace, Senghenydd
264. Joseph Thomas	33	214 Nantgarw Road, Caerphilly
265. Henry Thomas	44	9 Clive Street, Senghenydd
266. Richard John Davies	20	11 St Cenydd Terr, Penyrheol
267. Ernest Vranch	21	30 Cenydd Terrace, Senghenydd
268. William Davies	38	52 Commercial St, Senghenydd
269. Edward Rowlands	48	52 Dolyfelin Street, Caerphilly
270. Harry Abrahams	24	56 Coedcae Road, Abertridwr
271. David Williams	24	66 High Street, Abertridwr
272. Thomas John Jones	19	25 Bridgefield Street, Abertridwr
273. George David Anthony	17	60 Caerphilly Road, Senghenydd
274. Benjamin Joseph Priest	36	40 Ilan Road, Abertridwr
275. James Victor Priest	14	40 Ilan Road, Abertridwr
276. William John Taylor	33	28 Grove Terrace, Senghenydd
277. Harry Edwards	19	12 Tridwr Road, Abertridwr
278. Alfred Hugh Evans	18	60 High Street, Senghenydd
279. Fredk. Charles Parsons	22	47 Long Row, Nelson
280. Albert Wm. Henry Thorn	28	25 Parc Terrace, Senghenydd
281. James Edwards	42	12 Tridwr Road, Abertridwr
282. Robert John Symes	21	22 Graig Terrace, Senghenydd
283. Samuel Rowlands	28	11 Grove Terrace, Senghenydd
284. Richard Thomas	29	14 Ilan Road, Abertridwr
285. Hugh Jones	29	Oakfield House, Commercial St, Senghenydd
286. Thomas Benjamin Priest	16	40 Ilan Road, Abertridwr
287. William Evans	49	27 Grove Terrace, Senghenydd
288. Edwin Samuel Llewellyn	26	10 St Cenydd Terr, Penyrheol
289. Harry Copeland	33	22 St Cenydd Terr, Penyrheol

290. Thomas Edward Stanley	31	52 Commercial St, Senghenydd
291. Bertie Button	37	87 Ilan Road, Abertridwr
292. Harold Arthur Button	26	87 Ilan Road, Abertridwr
293. William Ingam	31	7 Universal Huts, Senghenydd
294. Walter Henley	27	190 Caerphilly Rd, Senghenydd
295. William John Harvey	28	8 Alexandra Terr, Senghenydd
296. Brynley Hyatt	22	51 Caerphilly Road, Senghenydd
297. Richard Charles Edwards	18	8 Coronation Terr, Senghenydd
298. William John Ross	22	22 Coronation Terr, Senghenydd
299. Harold Price	22	18 Woodland Terr, Senghenydd
300. John Lewis	35	17 Caerphilly Road, Senghenydd
301. Griffith Bowen	38	20 Parc Terrace, Senghenydd
302. Gomer Green	26	1 Grove Terrace, Senghenydd
303. Charles Baker	42	18 Alexandra Terr, Senghenydd
304. John Morgan	25	30 Stanley Street, Senghenydd
305. Patrick Sullivan	37	9 Station Terrace, Senghenydd
306. Idris Price	18	13 Clive Street, Senghenydd
307. Levi James Thomas	37	9 Parc Terrace, Senghenydd
308. John Williams	18	72 Caerphilly Road, Senghenydd
309. Thomas James	28	107 Commercial St, Senghenydd
310. Edwin Albert Victor Stanton	27	8 King Street, Abertridwr
311. Owen Morien John	22	10 Phillips Terrace, Senghenydd
312. David Morgan	29	66 Ilan Road, Abertridwr
313. Henry Kevil	33	77 Caerphilly Rd., Senghenydd
314. William John Jones	21	16 Grove Terrace, Senghenydd
315. *Unknown*		
316. Evan Evans	44	6 Grove Terrace, Senghenydd
317. Morgan Evans	59	9 Parc Terrace, Senghenydd
318. Ernest Petherick	16	15 Grove Terrace, Senghenydd
319. Samuel Bird	49	42 Commercial St., Senghenydd
320. Robert John Rowland	31	11 Grove Terrace, Senghenydd
321. Francis Simon Clarke	44	30 Woodland Terr., Senghenydd
322. Harry Davies	32	28 White Street, Caerphilly
323. Frank Pritchard	18	66 Caerphilly Road, Senghenydd
324. Henry Davies	33	167 High Street, Abertridwr
325. George Henry Evans	24	69 Caerphilly Rd., Senghenydd
326. Frederick Williams	43	72 Caerphilly Rd, Senghenydd
327. Henry Pritchard	29	66 Caerphilly Rd., Senghenydd
328. Ernest Edward Mulcock	21	28 White Street, Caerphilly

329.	John James Muldoon	17	Maesycarll, Penyrheol
330.	Thomas Edgar Jenkins	18	23 Dalton St, Cathays, Cardiff
331.	Thomas Lloyd Jones	37	16 Universal Huts, Senghenydd
332.	Evan Jones	52	152 Commercial St, Senghenydd
333.	James John Rosser	22	59 High Street, Senghenydd
334.	Edward Jones	50	131 Commercial St, Senghenydd
335.	William Evans	47	15 Coronation Terr, Senghenydd
336.	John Lynch	34	50 Cenydd Terrace, Senghenydd
337.	George Davies	30	4 Cwm Ceffyl Road, Abertridwr
338.	Morgan Edwards	16	61 Caerphilly Road, Senghenydd
339.	Alfred James Hadley	59	38 Stanley Street, Senghenydd
340.	Harry Field	32	2 Fields Park, Newbridge
341.	Richard Newell	23	87 Ilan Road, Abertridwr
342.	James Davies	49	20 Bradford Street, Caerphilly
343.	Robert James Davies	20	20 Bradford Street, Caerphilly
344.	Lewis Musty	42	8 Station Road, Senghenydd
345.	Samuel Curtis	25	8 Station Road, Senghenydd
346.	William Rowlands	59	51 Stanley Street, Senghenydd
347.	Rees Thomas	23	15 Bowls Terrace, Penyrheol
348.	Alfred Milton	15	15 Parc Terrace, Senghenydd
349.	Ruben Thomas Hughes	21	38 Stanley Street, Senghenydd
350.	Albert Edward McMahon	30	38 High Street, Abertridwr
351.	Josiah Morgan	25	66 Ilan Road, Abertridwr
352.	Daniel Kenvin	44	17 Graig Terrace, Senghenydd
353.	John Henry Benjamin	20	10 Church Road, Abertridwr
354.	Frank James Langmaid	17	44 Helen Street, Roath, Cardiff
355.	Thomas John Davies	26	74 Nantgarw Road, Caerphilly
356.	Richard Christopher Edwards	20	5 Phillips Terrace, Senghenydd
357.	Frederick Richards	32	22 Coronation Terr, Senghenydd
358.	William Ross	45	22 Coronation Terr, Senghenydd
359.	John Griffith Owen	24	58 High Street, Senghenydd
360.	Llewellyn Griffiths	32	11 Graig Terrace, Senghenydd
361.	William Leslie Wood	17	207 Caerphilly Rd., Senghenydd
362.	Richard David Rees	26	16 Woodland Terr., Senghenydd
363.	Samuel Jones	21	11 Graig Terrace, Senghenydd
364.	Arthur Joseph Gregory	20	7 Kingsley Place, Senghenydd
365.	George Owen	30	7 Cenydd Terrace, Senghenydd
366.	William Watkins	23	Gwalia Cottages, Bedwas Road, Caerphilly

367. John Roberts	31	Gwalia Cottages, Caerphilly
368. Francis Tooze	40	20 Cenydd Terrace, Senghenydd
369. James Druhan	26	20 Cenydd Terrace, Senghenydd
370. Humphrey Hughes	19	9 Stanley Street, Senghenydd
371. John Radcliffe	44	34 Grove Terrace, Senghenydd
372. Thomas Thomas	47	7 Woodland Terr., Senghenydd
373. Evan Twining	14	68 Commercial St, Senghenydd
374. Richard James	26	33 Cenydd Terrace, Senghenydd
375. John Edward Twining	28	68 Commercial St, Senghenydd
376. William Henry Morgan	15	228 Nantgarw Road, Caerphilly
377. Joseph Morgan	24	93 Ilan Road, Abertridwr
378. Charles Hall	36	1 Station Road, Senghenydd
379. James Edward Stephens	32	82 Ilan Road, Abertridwr
380. Thomas William Edwards	30	61 Caerphilly Road, Senghenydd
381. George Edwards	19	61 Caerphilly Road, Senghenydd
382. William David Evans	18	26 Parc Terrace, Senghenydd
383. Henry William Ford	28	25 Parc Terrace, Senghenydd
384. Thomas Jones	43	23 Bridgefield Street, Abertridwr
385. John Henry Jones	29	68 Caerphilly Road, Senghenydd
386. Samuel Baker	31	30 Parc Terrace, Senghenydd
387. Thomas Kinsey	25	202 Nantgarw Road, Caerphilly
388. John Kenvin	20	17 Graig Terrace, Senghenydd
389. James Herring	25	8 Phillips Terrace, Senghenydd
390. John Chapman	42	56 High Street, Senghenydd
391. Evan Thomas Rowlands	20	2 Windsor Terrace, Abertridwr
392. David Jenkins	17	23 Dalton Street, Cardiff
393. William John Phillips	20	164 Commercial St., Senghenydd
394. Albert Williams	23	93 Ilan Road, Abertridwr
395. Thomas Davies	43	37 Graig Terrace, Senghenydd
396. Alfred Rees Tudor	14	33 Alexandra Terr, Senghenydd
397. David John Davies	29	124 Commercial St, Senghenydd
398. Joseph Wright	33	17 Phillips Terrace, Senghenydd
399. Thomas Philip Thomas	21	165 Commercial St. Senghenydd
400. James Smith	31	7 Brynhyfryd Terr, Senghenydd
401. Henry Francis Davies	25	8 Station Road, Senghenydd
402. Hugh Hughes	22	9 Stanley Street, Senghenydd
403. James Twining	16	68 Commercial St., Senghenydd
404. William Davies	43	33 Alexandra Terr, Senghenydd
405. George Ernest Spreadbury	32	31 Alexandra Terr, Senghenydd

406. David Hughes	49	84 Thomas Street, Abertridwr
407. Robert Garfield Roberts	20	Mabon Cottage, Groeswen
408. Evan William Jones	27	18 Cenydd Terrace, Senghenydd
409. William Jones	29	1 Woodland Terrace, Senghenydd
410. Evan Jones	53	171 Commercial St, Senghenydd
411. James Scriven	45	19 Clive Street, Senghenydd
412. William Davies	36	67 Caerphilly Road, Senghenydd
413. George Edwards	48	38 High Street, Senghenydd
414. Frank Hollister	20	18 Brynhyfryd Terr, Senghenydd
415. Harry Penny	27	22 St Cenydd Terr, Penyrheol
416. John Davies	27	21 Station Terrace, Senghenydd
417. Ellis Davies	22	4 Cwm Ceffyl Road, Abertridwr
418. Thomas Tucker	21	52 Stanley Street, Senghenydd
419. *Unknown*		
420. Archibald Williams	19	164 Commercial St, Senghenydd

Note on the Cause of Death as found at the Inquest

The inquest recorded that all 422 persons listed died from one or other of nine separate causes. These, with the number of deaths, were as follows:-

Cause of Death	*Number of Deaths*
Suffocation	74
Burns and Suffocation	251
Burns, Injuries and Suffocation	58
Injury and Suffocation	10
Wounds and Suffocation	1
Burns and Shock	4
Burns, Injury and Shock	13
Burns, Exhaustion and Shock	1
Injury and Shock	10
Total	**422**

Footnote

In his evidence at the inquest Doctor James said that the use of the term 'suffocation' called for explanation. Its use in the majority of deaths should be taken to mean poisoning by carbon monoxide and not suffocation in the sense of asphyxiation.

Redmayne also pointed out that, in respect of a number of the bodies found in the Kimberley, Mafeking and Pretoria Districts which were described as being burnt as well as suffocated, he was of the opinion that this was an error in description. Some of the bodies so described were discovered in places where he had found no indication of the roadways having been traversed by flame. He felt the bodies had been treated as burned due to their being found, some weeks after the explosion, in a blackened condition. He thought this was probably due to the effect of coal dust and mortification.

LIST B

Taken from the Appendix to the Official Report of the Inquiry (Cd 7346)

	Name	*Age*	*Address*
1.	Charles Brown	31	23 Caerphilly Rd, Senghenydd
2.	George Chant	34	35 Grove Terrace, Senghenydd
3.	Fred French	21	2 Gelli Terrace, Senghenydd
4.	Richard Jones	36	28 High Street, Senghenydd
5.	Henry Jones	33	2 School Street, Senghenydd
6.	William Jones	40	114 Ilan Road, Abertridwr
7.	Gilbert Jones	24	26 High Street, Abertridwr
8.	Drychan Jones	22	4 Hendre, Abertridwr
9.	William Jenkins	21	186 Cairn Street, Cardiff
10.	William Kin	25	25 Cenydd Terrace, Senghenydd
11.	William Henry Morgan	33	12 Woodland Terr, Senghenydd
12.	David Lewis Morgan	35	37 Bowls Terrace, Penyrheol
13.	George A. Price	28	137 High Street, Abertridwr
14.	Lewis Rees	41	34 Station Terrace, Senghenydd
15.	William Sullivan	35	52 St Cenydd Terr, Penyrheol
16.	William O. Williams	22	55 High Street, Senghenydd
17.	Simeon Worman	57	Windsor Place, Senghenydd
18.	Job Williams	52	8 High Street, Abertridwr
19.	Richard Williams	43	28 Stanley Street, Senghenydd

LIST C

Compiled from Newspaper Reports

1.	William Henry Robson	—	4 Minny Street, Cardiff
2.	David Jones	—	6 Cenydd Terrace, Senghenydd
3.	George Smale	—	Thomas Street, Abertridwr

APPENDIX III

Persons rescued — from the Bottanic District, near pit bottom and the West York District — on 14/15 October 1913

BOTTANIC DISTRICT

Name	*Address*
1. George Moore (father)	174 Bedwas Road, Caerphilly
2. Evan James Moore (son)	174 Bedwas Road, Caerphilly
3. George Moore (son)	174 Bedwas Road, Caerphilly
4. James Hill	15 Brynhyfryd Terrace, Senghenydd
5. Bert Williams	9 Grove Terrace, Senghenydd
6. John Owen Jones	183 Caerphilly Road, Senghenydd
7. Archibald Dean	204 Nantgarw Road, Caerphilly
8. Arthur Balsom	17 Corbett Crescent, Caerphilly
9. Trevor Morgan	Black Cock, Caerphilly
10. Wilf Vizzard	15 Alexandra Terrace, Senghenydd
11. Ernest Jones	141 Commercial Street, Senghenydd
12. Joe Evans	20 Stanley Street, Senghenydd
13. Charles Steel	18 Station Terrace, Senghenydd
14. William Jones	Coronation Terrace, Senghenydd
15. Benjamin David	159 Commercial St, Senghenydd
16. Benjamin Hill	Parc Terrace, Senghenydd
17. William Jones	65 High Street, Senghenydd
18. Evan Jones	183 Caerphilly Rd., Senghenydd

WEST YORK DISTRICT

19. William Henry Lasbury	*Address not quoted* — but probably 15 Graig Terrace, Senghenydd (Occupation: Assistant Timberman)

Near pit bottom at the Lancaster Shaft

20. Ernest Moses	*Address not quoted* (Occupation: Shackler)

Bibliography

Legislation

Coal Mines Regulation Act 1887. CH 58 50 and 51 Vict.

Workmen's Compensation Act 1897. CH 37 60 and 61 Vict.

Coal Mines Act 1911. CH 50 1 and 2 Geo 5.

Government Publications

Reports to H.M. Secretary of State for the Home Department on the circumstances attending an explosion at the Universal Colliery, Glamorgan, on 24th May 1901 by W. Galloway FGS; S. T. Evans KC MP and J. T. Robson. (Cd 947)

H.M. Inspector of Mines Reports for 1901 and 1913 to 1914.

Report of the Departmental Committee on the Use of Electricity in Coal Mines — 1904. (Cd 1916)

Report to H.M. Secretary of State for the Home Department on the disaster which occurred at Courrieres Mine, Pas de Calais, France, on 10th March 1906. (Cd 3171)

Reports of the Royal Commission on Mines:
First Report — 30th May 1907. (Cd 3548)
Second Report — July 1909. (Cd 4820)
Third Report — February 1911. (Cd 5561)

Report of the Departmental Committee appointed to consider the working of the existing Special Rules for the Use of Electricity in Mines — 1911. (Cd 5498)

Reports to the Rt. Hon. the Secretary of State for the Home Department on the causes and circumstances attending the explosion which occurred at the Senghenydd Colliery on Tuesday, 14th October 1913, by R. A. S. Redmayne, CB, H.M. Chief Inspector of Mines (Commissioner) and Evan Williams, Chairman of the South Wales and Monmouthshire Coalowners' Association, and Robert Smillie, President of the Miners' Federation of Great Britain (Assessors). (Cd 7346)

Arnot, R. Page	The South Wales Miners — A History of the South Wales Miners' Federation (1898–1914)	1967
	The Miners: A History of the Miners' Federation of Great Britain (1889–1914)	1949
	Years of Struggle	1953
Cymmrodorion, The Honourable Society of	Dictionary of Welsh Biography	1959
Duckham, Helen and Baron	Great Pit Disasters — Great Britain 1700 to the present day	
Edwards, Ness	History of the South Wales Miners	1926
	History of the South Wales Miners' Federation	1938
Galloway, Robert L.	Annals of Coal Mining and the Coal Trade First Series	1898
	Second Series	1904
	A History of Coal Mining in Great Britain *(Edited by Helen and Baron Duckham)* —	1969
Griffin, A. R.	Coal Mining	1971
Jevons, H. Stanley	The British Coal Trade	1915
Phillips, Elizabeth	A History of the Pioneers of the Welsh Coalfield	1925
Redmayne, R. A. S.	Men, Mines and Memories	1942
Rees, William	Cardiff – A History of the City	1969
Thompson, Herbert M.	Cardiff	1936
Wilkins, Charles	The South Wales Coal Trade and its Allied Industries	1888
	History of the Iron, Steel and Tinplate Trades	

Other Documents

Transcript of Proceedings before David Rees Esq, Coroner at the Inquest on the bodies of the men who lost their lives at the Universal Colliery, Senghenydd in the County of Glamorgan on the 14th October 1913.

Registers of the Clerk to the Justices for the Petty Sessions for the Division of Caerphilly Lower — for 1914, 1915 and 1916.

A History of Senghenydd up to 1918 by J. B. Phillips BA

Newspapers

Western Mail; South Wales Echo; Merthyr Express; The Times; Illustrated London News; Daily Sketch; Daily Mirror.

Index